MYSTERY PLAYS

8 Plays for the Classroom
Based On Stories
by Famous Writers

Adapted by Tom Conklin

SCHOLASTIC
PROFESSIONAL BOOKS

New York • Toronto • London • Auckland • Sydney

DEDICATION

To Dan, who introduced me to Sherlock Holmes and Sam Spade.

ACKNOWLEDGMENTS

AS SIMPLE AS ABC by Ellery Queen is adapted and reprinted by permission of the author's estate and the author's agents, Scott Meredith Literary Agency, L.P., 845 Third Avenue, New York, New York, 10022.

THE TENTH CLEW by Dashiell Hammett is adapted and reprinted by permission of the trustees of the estate of Dashiell Hammett.

Cover design by Vincent Ceci and Jaime Lucero
Cover illustration by Mona Mark
Interior design by Joy Jackson Childs
Interior illustrations by Ron Zalme

ISBN 0-590-20939-6

TABLE OF CONTENTS

▼▼▼▼▼▼▼▼▼▼▼▼▼▼▼▼▼▼▼▼▼▼▼▼▼

INTRODUCTION

WE'D LIKE TO KNOW
WHAT YOU THINK!

Scholastic Professional Books is committed to providing teachers with great teaching ideas that meet the needs of their students. Let us know what you think. How did you use the plays in this book? Which plays did your students enjoy the most? You can write to us at:

Mystery Plays
Scholastic Professional Books
555 Broadway
New York, New York 10012

INTRODUCTION

▼ ▼ ▼ ▼ ▼ ▼ ▼ ▼ ▼ ▼ ▼ ▼ ▼ ▼ ▼ ▼ ▼ ▼ ▼

Looking for thrills, chills, or an intriguing puzzle to challenge your mind? Scan the bestseller lists and you will find mystery stories at or near the top. Visit your local cineplex, and the odds are that you can see at least one crime story or mystery thriller. Turn on your TV, and you always are sure to find a detective story being shown somewhere on the cable dial.

Without a doubt, the mystery genre is one of the most popular forms of story-telling in the world. What's more, the fun and excitement of mystery stories offer a great way to introduce young people to the pleasures of reading. That's why we have gathered eight classic stories of crime and detection in this volume of plays.

Mystery stories have a respected literary pedigree. The first mysteries were written more than 100 years ago, by Romantic authors like Edgar Allan Poe and Nathaniel Hawthorne. The genre evolved through the works of Victorian authors like Sir Arthur Conan Doyle. By the 1920s and 1930s, the mystery story was thoroughly established as a popular standard. With the growth of movies, radio, television, and other mass media, mysteries became a popular habit for millions of people.

The plays in this book have been carefully selected to give your students a broad exposure to the roots of the genre, and a sampling of the most common forms of mystery stories. Here you will find tales of blackmail and con artists, hardboiled murders and elaborate whodunits, along with introductions to some of the world's favorite detectives.

Once your students have read or performed these plays, encourage them to investigate their local library or bookstore for more mystery stories. There are countless mysteries in print, with detectives and situations to suit every taste.

So, get ready for mystery. Or, as Sherlock Holmes would say, "the game is afoot!"

RAPPACCINI'S DAUGHTER

By Nathaniel Hawthorne

Introduction

Femme fatale is another expression for "dangerous woman." Mystery stories are filled with beautiful women who lead men to their doom. What femme fatale could be more dangerous than Poison Ivy, the villain from "Batman" comics, whose very kiss is deadly?

Believe it or not, "Poison Ivy" is a version of a character invented 150 years ago by the author Nathaniel Hawthorne. That character — Rappaccini's daughter — leads a young man named Giovanni to a fate worse than death....

Characters

Giovanni, *a young man*

Lisabetta, *his landlady*

Pietro, *an old man, and a friend of Giovanni's father*

Rappaccini, *a withered old man*

Beatrice, *Rappaccini's daughter — a beautiful young woman*

Narrator

Scene One

Narrator: Very long ago, a young man named Giovanni left the country and came to the city to study at the university. Giovanni, without much money in his pocket, finds lodging in a gloomy room in an old building. As he first enters the room with Lisabetta, his landlady, Giovanni sighs loudly.

Lisabetta: My goodness! What a sigh to come out of a young man's heart! Do you find this house gloomy? For the love of heaven, then, put your head out of the window and you will see bright sunshine.

Narrator: Giovanni mechanically does as the old woman advised. The sunshine falls into a beautiful garden in a courtyard beneath the window.

Giovanni: Does this garden belong to the house?

Lisabetta: Heaven forbid! No, that garden is grown by the famous doctor Rappaccini, who lives next door. It is said that he turns those plants into potent medicines. You may often see the doctor hard at work in the garden. Sometimes you will find his daughter, Beatrice, there, too.

Narrator: After Lisabetta leaves, Giovanni stares down into the beautiful garden. Soon, a tall, thin, sallow, sickly-looking man comes into the garden.

Giovanni: That must be Rappaccini!

Narrator: The old man intently studies every shrub and flower along the garden path. But he does not touch or smell any of the plants. He wears heavy gloves as he picks the weeds from the flower beds. Then he approaches a large, beautiful bush in the heart of the garden. The bush is covered with lush, purple flowers. As he nears the bush, Rappaccini puts a mask over his nose and mouth, as if to avoid any scent from the plant. He gingerly touches the plant, then pulls back.

Rappaccini (*calling*)**:** Beatrice! Beatrice!

Beatrice (*off*)**:** Here I am, father! Where are you? In the garden?

Rappaccini: Yes, Beatrice. And I need your help.

Narrator: Giovanni gasps in awe as a beautiful young woman enters the garden. She is dressed in a flowing purple gown, the same color as the flowers on the bush next to old Rappaccini.

Rappaccini: Here, Beatrice. Our most treasured plant needs tender care. But, as old and frail as I am, I'm afraid that handling it would prove fatal to me. From now on I leave it entirely in your care.

Beatrice: And I will gladly tend it.

Narrator: Giovanni rubs his eyes in disbelief as Beatrice gathers the flowering boughs in her arms and inhales their perfume. In the evening light, it is hard to tell where the lush purple plant ends and the young woman begins.

Giovanni: Is it a woman tending a flower? Or is it one sister giving her loving attention to another?

Scene Two

Narrator: The next day, Giovanni visits an old friend of his father named Pietro Baglioni.

Giovanni: Pietro, what do you know of a doctor named Rappaccini?

Pietro: He is very skilled. Still, there are things about him that are not right. . .

Giovanni: Yes? and what are they?

Pietro (*smiling*)**:** Do you have a disease of the body or heart that makes you ask about the good doctor? Rappaccini is a learned man — yet he cares more for science than for people. Patients are interesting to him only as subjects for experiments. He would sacrifice any human being in order to gain more knowledge.

Giovanni: That is terrible indeed. And yet, Pietro, isn't it noble, too? Are there many people with such a passion for science?

Pietro: Heaven forbid! Or, if people do love science, let us hope they have sounder views than Rappaccini.

Giovanni: What are his views?

Pietro: He believes that all disease may be cured by applying doses of what we call poison. He even grows a garden filled with poisonous plants that he uses in his experiments. He loves his garden — and his experiments — more than anything in this world.

Giovanni: I don't know how much this doctor may love science. But I do know that there must be one object more dear to him — his daughter.

Pietro *(laughing)*: Aha! Your secret is out. You have heard about Beatrice. All of the young men in town are wild about her, but few have ever seen her face. She keeps entirely to Rappaccini's house and garden. But they say that she knows as much about her father's work as old Rappaccini himself. . . .

Scene Three

Narrator: Giovanni leaves Pietro and returns to his room. Along the way, he stops to buy a bouquet of flowers. When he returns to his room, the shadows of evening are falling in the garden. Beatrice walks up and down the garden path.

Giovanni *(watching)*: She is the most lovely woman on Earth.

Narrator: Giovanni watches as Beatrice stops at the beautiful bush covered with purple flowers.

Beatrice *(to the plant)*: Give me your breath, dear sister. *(She sniffs the flowers of the plant.)* And give me one of your flowers.

Narrator: Beatrice plucks a flower from the bush. Giovanni watches as a few drops from the flower's stem fall to the garden path and onto the back of a small orange lizard resting at Beatrice's feet. The lizard thrashes around violently, then falls silent. The animal is dead.

Giovanni *(startled)*: Am I awake or dreaming? What shall I call this woman — is she beautiful? Or horrible?

Narrator: Beatrice strolls through the garden. As she passes near Giovanni's window, a beautiful butterfly flutters near her head. Giovanni watches, horrified, as the butterfly falls to the ground, dead. Beatrice, noticing the butterfly, looks up. She sees Giovanni staring down at her.

Giovanni *(tossing down his bouquet of flowers)*: Signora, these are pure and healthful flowers. Take them for my sake — the sake of Giovanni.

Beatrice: Thank you, Giovanni. I accept your gift. I would like to give you this purple flower of mine in exchange. However, I can't throw the flower all the way to your window, so you will have to be satisfied with my thanks.

Narrator: Beatrice walks down the path and into Rappaccini's house.

Giovanni *(to himself)*: I don't believe it. . . . It can't be true! As she left the garden, my bouquet of flowers seemed to wilt in her hand.

Scene Four

Narrator: Days later, Giovanni walks down the street.

Pietro *(calling)*: Giovanni! My friend! Wait for me!

Giovanni *(hurrying)*: I must get back to my rooms.

Pietro: What — you don't have time for me? We must have a word or two.

Giovanni: Oh, all right. But quickly! Quickly!

Narrator: At that moment, an old, sallow figure passes by.

Pietro *(to the man)*: Ah. Good day, sir.

Rappaccini: Good day. *(He stares at Giovanni.)* Hmmm. Very interesting. Very interesting, indeed. *(He leaves.)*

Pietro *(horrified)*: That was old Rappaccini. He knows you!

Giovanni: How could he? We've never met!

Pietro: I tell you, he knows you! He is making a study of you — I am certain. He looked at you the same way he looks at a rat in a cage — or an insect pinned to board. You are one of Rappaccini's experiments!

Giovanni *(angry)*: Will you make a fool of me? That would be a terrible experiment! *(He marches off.)*

Pietro: I'm afraid for my young friend. So he has never met Rappaccini? What of Rappaccini's daughter?

Narrator: When Giovanni returns to his room, Lisabetta is waiting there.

Lisabetta: Signor! I have found a private entrance into the garden below your window.

Giovanni: What's that? A private entrance?

Lisabetta: Hush! Not so loud. Many a young man in town would pay dearly for this knowledge. Every young man wants to . . . smell the flowers.

Giovanni (*handing her a gold coin*): Show me the way.

Scene Five

Narrator: Minutes later, Giovanni walks through a door hidden in the wall directly below his window. He is in the garden. The plants, as he looks closely at them, seem wild, beautiful—and almost unnatural. As he studies the plants, Giovanni hears a rustle of fabric. He turns to finds Beatrice watching him.

Beatrice (*smiling slightly*): Sir, you love flowers. No wonder my father's rare collection has tempted you here. If he were here, he could tell you all about the many plants here.

Giovanni: There are those who say you know as much about the garden as your father.

Beatrice: Are there such rumors? I have grown up in this garden, and know all about these plants' colors and smells. But don't believe what you may have heard about me as a scientist. I am not like my father.

Narrator: Beatrice and Giovanni spend hours walking through the garden, admiring the beauty of the flowers and their deep, sickly-sweet smell. It is almost night when they come to the purple-flowered bush in the center of the garden.

Beatrice (*to the plant*): Ah! Sister! For the first time ever I have forgotten about you!

Giovanni: Lady, once you offered me one of the flowers from this bush. Let me take one now.

Narrator: Beatrice shrieks as Giovanni reaches to pluck a flower from the bush.

Beatrice: Do not touch it! Not for your life! It is fatal!

Narrator: Beatrice turns and runs into Rappaccini's house. On her way she passes her father, who stands in the doorway staring coldly at Giovanni, a tiny smile on his thin lips.

Giovanni (*to himself*): How long has he been watching — and why?

Scene Six

Narrator: Giovanni returned to the garden the next day. And the day after . . . and the day after that. He felt love taking root in his heart. Soon, his visits with Beatrice are all that he lives for. One morning, Giovanni has an unexpected visit from old Pietro.

Pietro (*sniffing the air*): What a strange smell is in the air. It is sweet — yet I don't like it. It is as if the scent will make me sick. Are you wearing a cologne?

Giovanni: No. It must be your imagination.

Pietro: My young friend, have you been seeing Beatrice?

Giovanni: What if I have?

Pietro: You must listen to me. I know her better than you do. I know what she is better than you.

Giovanni: And what is she?

Pietro: Poison. Her father has raised her among his poisonous plants — as an experiment. And now . . . he is including you in the experiment.

Giovanni: No! No, it can't be true.

Pietro: Don't despair. Take this bottle of medicine. It contains a powerful antidote. The most lethal poison in the world will be cured with the liquid in this bottle.

Narrator: Pietro puts the bottle on a table and goes out of the room, leaving Giovanni alone with his fears.

Giovanni (*to himself*): It can't be true. How can a person be poisonous? It's a fairy tale and I will prove it.

Narrator: Giovanni leaves his room and goes to a flower shop. He buys a beautiful bouquet and takes it back to his room.

Giovanni: I'll conduct my own experiment. I will give these flowers to Beatrice. Then, when they do not fade in her presence, I will know that old Pietro is filled with hatred for Rappaccini, and not knowledge about his daughter.

Narrator: Giovanni stares at his reflection in a mirror. A gentle breeze blows through the window by him and onto the bouquet at his side.

Giovanni (*smiling*): At least I am not "poisonous."

Narrator: Giovanni gasps in horror. In the mirror, he sees the beautiful flowers at his side shrivel up and die.

Giovanni (*to himself, in panic*): Didn't Pietro say he noticed a strange aroma in the room? Could — could it have come from me? Am I turning as poisonous as the flowers in the garden?

Narrator: A quiet voice comes through the window.

Beatrice: Giovanni? Giovanni, where are you? Come down. I am waiting in the garden.

Scene Seven

Narrator: Giovanni goes down to the garden. Beatrice stands by the bush of purple flowers in the center of the garden.

Giovanni: Beatrice, where did this plant come from?

Beatrice: My father created it.

Giovanni: He created it?

Beatrice: Yes. He knows all about the flowers and plants of the world. This bush sprouted on the very day I was born. I have spent every day of my life in its presence.

Giovanni: It is poison.

Beatrice (*quietly*): I know. And it has been a lonely life. Until you entered the garden.

Giovanni: And now I am poisonous, too! Like you, I am doomed to spend my life in this garden, sealed off from the world.

Beatrice: No. It can't be!

Giovanni: No? Watch the power I have gained from you.

Narrator: A swarm of insects flits through the air. Giovanni walks to them and blows gently into the swarm. The insects fall to the ground, dead.

Beatrice (*in horror*): I see. I see! But Giovanni, it is due to my father's science, not me! Please don't blame me. Not for all the world would I have harmed you.

Narrator: She turns away, weeping. Giovanni comes to her side.

Giovanni: Dearest Beatrice — there is still hope.

Narrator: Giovanni takes from his pocket the bottle Pietro gave him.

Giovanni: This bottle holds powerful medicine. It can cure the foulest poisons. Please take the medicine. Together, we can leave this terrible place.

Beatrice: Give it to me! I will take it. But — wait until I have tried it before you drink from it, my love.

Narrator: Beatrice drinks deeply from the bottle. Just then, Rappaccini appears in the garden.

Rappaccini: Daughter! You are no longer alone in this world. Pluck a flower from your sister, that your new husband may carry it with him. You two shall pass through this life together. Together — and alone.

Beatrice (*weakly*): Father, why did you do this to me? Why did you inflict this misery on your child?

Rappaccini: Misery? What do you mean, "misery?" You are the most powerful creature on earth! You can destroy any living thing with a single breath.

Beatrice *(sinking to the ground)***:** I would have rather been loved than feared. But it's over now. The evil you have done will pass away, like the scent of these beautiful and deadly flowers.

Narrator: Beatrice dies at her father's feet. Giovanni falls to her side, weeping. A powerful voice calls from the window of Giovanni's room.

Pietro: Rappaccini! Your poison was so powerful it became part of your daughter's very being! To destroy the poison, she had to die as well.

Narrator: He points at the dead woman next to the bush of poisonous purple flowers.

Pietro: Behold! This is the result of your grand experiment!

Nathaniel Hawthorne...

...was born July 4, 1804, in Salem, Massachusetts. His father, a sea captain, died when Nathaniel was four years old, and the boy was raised by his mother's family. He attended Bowdoin College, where he became friends with future U.S. President Franklin Pierce and fellow author Henry Wadsworth Longfellow. Hawthorne began writing fiction while still a student. As a young man, he edited one of the nation's first magazines, the *American Magazine of Useful and Entertaining Knowledge*.

Hawthorne's first collection of short stories, *Twice Told Tales,* was published in 1837. In 1846 he published another collection of stories *Mosses from an Old Manse*, which included "Rappaccini's Daughter." Hawthorne's masterpiece, the novel *The Scarlet Letter*, secured his place in American literature when it was published in 1850. Upon the election of his old friend Franklin Pierce to the presidency, Hawthorne was appointed U.S. consul to Liverpool, which gave him the opportunity to travel throughout Europe.

Hawthorne died on May 19, 1864, in Plymouth, New Hampshire.

FURTHER READING

Students who enjoyed this story may also wish to read Hawthorne's short story collections: *Twice Told Tales* and *Mosses from an Old Manse*.

Paul Fleischman's *Grave Images: Three Stories*, a Newbery Honor book, may also appeal to students who enjoyed this play. Fleischman's writing style has been compared to that of Hawthorne and Edgar Allan Poe.

Ambitious, older students looking for other Romantic tales of passion and intrigue may want to read *Jane Eyre* by Charlotte Bronte and *Wuthering Heights* by her sister Emily. Although not technically mysteries, these novels have many of the elements of a good mystery story.

ACTIVITIES

All For Science?

Rappaccini was completely dedicated to science. In an attempt to discover the secrets of diseases, he was willing to sacrifice the lives of his own daughter and her friend Giovanni. Was Rappaccini justified in what he did? Let students have a class debate in which one side takes Rappaccini's side — that scientific knowledge is worth any human suffering it may cause. The other side should take the side of old Pietro, who thinks that Rappaccini went too far in his pursuit of knowledge.

Isolation

In "Rappaccini's Daughter," Beatrice and Giovanni are isolated from the rest of society by Rappaccini's experiment. Have students imagine that Beatrice survived and that she and Giovanni lived together to a ripe old age. Students should assume either the role of Giovanni or Beatrice as an old person, and write a brief essay, describing their thoughts of living a life of isolation. What were the worse things about it? Were there any benefits?

My Mystery

"Rappaccini's Daughter" is a variation on the classic "mad scientist" theme. Have students write their own mystery story featuring a mad scientist and a modern scientific topic, such as:

◆ cloning
◆ animal lab testing
◆ environmental pollution

THE PURLOINED LETTER

By Edgar Allan Poe

Introduction

Blackmail! The word itself sounds mysterious and dangerous.

What's your deepest, darkest secret? Imagine that your worst enemy found it out. And imagine that your enemy used that secret against you — do as they tell you, or your enemy will tell the world your secret. That's blackmail — and mystery writers use it in their plots all the time.

Published in 1845, this classic story of blackmail is one the first detective stories ever written. It contains a stolen letter, an evil, ambitious politician, and M. Dupin, the first detective in the history of literature. See if you can crack the case of the purloined letter along with Dupin.

Characters

Dupin, *a private detective in Paris*
Edgar, *Dupin's best friend*
Prefect of Police, *the head of the Paris police force*
King, *the ruler of France*
Queen, *the King's young wife*
Minister D., *a scoundrel who works for the King*
Narrator, *the Narrator is Edgar, looking back on what happened*

Scene One

Narrator: Just after dark one gusty autumn evening, I was enjoying a visit with my friend, C. August Dupin. As we sat in silence, the door was thrown open and in came our old acquaintance, the Prefect of the police.

Dupin *(standing)*: Greetings, my friend! Have a seat while I light the lamps. To what do we owe the honor of this visit?

Prefect: I have come to ask your opinion on something, Dupin. It's official business that is causing me a great deal of trouble.

Dupin *(sitting)*: Ah! If it is anything requiring thought, we should discuss it while sitting in the dark.

Prefect *(chuckling)*: Now, there's another one of your odd notions!

Narrator: The Prefect called everything "odd" that was beyond his own comprehension. He lived in a world full of "oddities."

Edgar: What is the difficulty now? A murder?

Prefect: Oh no, nothing like that. The fact is, the mystery is very simple indeed. I don't doubt that we can solve it ourselves. But, then I thought Dupin would like to hear the details of the case, because it is so . . . well . . . odd.

Dupin: A mystery that is simple and odd.

Prefect: Why, yes. And not exactly that, either. The fact is, we have been puzzled because the mystery is so simple, yet it has us baffled.

Dupin: Perhaps it is the simplicity of the case which baffles you.

Prefect *(laughing)*: What nonsense!

Dupin: Perhaps the mystery is a little too plain. . . .

Prefect *(laughing harder)*: Oh, good heavens! Who ever heard of such an idea?

Dupin: . . . A little too self-evident.

Prefect *(laughing hysterically)*: Ha! Ha! Ha! Oh, Dupin, you will be the death of me yet!

Edgar: And what are the facts of this mystery?

Prefect: I will tell you. But, before I begin, let me caution you that this case demands the greatest secrecy. I would lose my job if anyone found out I told you about the case.

Edgar: Proceed.

Dupin: Or not.

Prefect: Well then, here are the facts. . . .

Scene Two

Narrator: The Prefect told us his story. It started a few months before, when the Queen of France received a letter. She was reading it, alone in the royal rooms, when the King entered.

King: My dear, what is that you are reading?

Queen *(startled)*: This? Oh, it is nothing! *(to herself)* He must not read this letter! It contains my personal secrets — things that the King must never know!

Narrator: The Queen began to hide the letter in a drawer, then decided it best to simply toss it onto her desk, so as not to arouse suspicion. At that instant, Minister D. entered the room.

Minister D. *(bowing)*: Your majesties, thank you for seeing me. I have a few matters of business to discuss.

King: You may proceed.

Minister D.: Thank you. But, her majesty the Queen seems nervous.

Queen *(eyeing the letter)*: Oh, it is nothing.

Minister D. *(following her glance)*: I see.

Narrator: Minister D., being a bold scoundrel, immediately saw that the letter was important to the Queen. What is more, he could see that she wished to hide it from the King. Minister D. placed a letter he had brought with him onto the desk next to the Queen's letter, then began discussing business. After fifteen minutes or so, he deliberately picked up the Queen's letter, leaving his own.

Queen *(gasping)*: No!

Minister D.: Is something wrong, your highness?

King: What is it, dear?

Queen: Oh . . . er. . . nothing.

Minister D. *(smiling with malice)*: Very good. I will leave you now. *(bowing to the King)* Good day, your majesty. *(bowing to the Queen)* Your highness, I'm sure we will talk soon.

Scene Three

Edgar: So it's blackmail!

Prefect: Exactly. Minister D. has the letter. He threatens to give it to the King, unless the Queen does just as he asks. Minister D. has used his power to gain political advantage. The Queen is desperate to get the letter back, and has given the job to me.

Dupin: And no better detective could be desired — or even imagined.

Prefect: You flatter me — but it is possible that was her majesty's opinion.

Edgar: Is it certain that Minister D. still has the letter?

Prefect: He must. For his blackmail to work, he must be in a position to show the King the letter immediately. If he had already done so, I am sure that all of Paris would know!

Edgar: But you are quite skilled in these investigations. You have done this sort of thing often before.

Prefect: Oh, yes. And for this reason I had great hopes. Minister D. is seldom home at night. I have keys, as you know, which can open any room or cabinet in Paris. For the past three months we have been busy ransacking Minister D.'s apartment. To no avail — we have not found the letter.

Edgar: Is it possible that Minister D. is carrying the letter with him?

Prefect: No. Three times I have had patrolmen waylay Minister D. and search him. He did not have the letter with him.

Dupin: You could have spared yourself the trouble. The Minister is not altogether a fool, and would have expected these searches.

Prefect: Perhaps he is not a fool, but then he's a poet, which is almost the same thing.

Dupin *(smiling)*: True . . . although I have been guilty of writing verse myself.

Edgar: Did you thoroughly search Minister D.'s apartment?

Prefect: Of course! We took our time and searched everywhere. We opened every possible drawer. . .

Edgar: How about "secret" drawers?

Prefect: There is no such thing to the trained eye. We probed the furniture cushions with long needles. We carefully took apart the tables and chairs —

Edgar: Why on earth did you do that?

Prefect: A letter could be hidden in a hollow leg or under the top of a table or seat of a chair.

Dupin: Was this letter hidden in that fashion?

Prefect: No. We put the furniture back together. Then we looked behind mirrors and pictures, in the mattress and bed clothes, behind curtains and under carpets. Then we searched the building itself. We divided its surface into sections, which we numbered. We examined every square inch with a microscope, searching for a secret compartment. Then we searched the houses on either side of Minister D.'s house.

Edgar: The two other houses! You have had a great deal of trouble!

Prefect *(blushing)*: Yes. But her majesty has offered a substantial reward.

Edgar: Reward or no, you have not found the letter. You must be mistaken in thinking Minister D. has it in his rooms.

Prefect: I am afraid you're right. Dupin, what do you think I should do?

Dupin: Keep looking.

Prefect: Is that the best advice you can give?

Dupin *(shrugging his shoulders)*: As you said, the letter must be somewhere close at hand. You simply haven't found it yet. Do you have a description of the letter?

Prefect *(sighing)*: Yes, I do.

Narrator: The Prefect took out a notebook and proceeded to read a detailed description of the missing document. After he finished reading the description, he left, more depressed than I had ever seen him before.

Scene Four

Narrator: About a month later the Prefect paid us another visit.

Edgar: Well, Prefect, what about the purloined letter? Did you find it?

Prefect: No, confound it, although I followed Dupin's advice and re-searched Minister D.'s rooms. It was wasted time, as I knew it would be.

Dupin: How much was the reward offered, did you say?

Prefect: Why, quite a lot. I — er — I hesitate to say exactly how much. But it's big enough that I would gladly write a check in the amount of 50,000 francs to anyone who could give me the letter.

Dupin: In that case, get out your checkbook. When you have signed a check to me for that amount, I will give you the letter.

Narrator: I was astounded. The Prefect was absolutely thunderstruck. He stared silently at my friend, then took out his checkbook, wrote a check for 50,000 francs, and handed it to Dupin. My friend studied it carefully for a moment, slipped it into his pocketbook, then unlocked his desk drawer. He took out a letter and handed it to the Prefect.

Prefect *(his eyes popping out)*: But — but — how?!

Narrator: Then, without another word, the Prefect rushed out of our rooms with the letter.

Dupin: The police are very able . . . in their way. Unfortunately, they are no brighter or stupider than the mass of people. Their investigations often fail when they encounter a criminal smarter than they are — and often when they deal with criminals who are not as smart.

Edgar: But they conducted a thorough search!

Dupin: Of course. But they searched in places where they, themselves, might have hidden the letter! They did not think that Minister D., who is no fool, would anticipate that his rooms would be searched. Of course, he would never hide the letter behind a mirror, or in a hollow table leg, because if he did it would certainly be found. He would choose a simpler place to hide it. In fact — he would choose not to hide it at all!

Edgar: I think I understand your reasoning. But how did you manage to get hold of the letter?

Dupin: It was simple. I took it!

Scene Five

Narrator: Dupin told me how he paid a visit to Minister D. himself.

Minister D. *(yawning)*: Why, hello, Dupin. What brings you to my rooms?

Dupin: I was in the neighborhood and thought I would stop in for a chat.

Minister D.: Come in, my friend. It is good to see you. But why are you wearing dark glasses?

Dupin: My eyes are tired and the light bothers them.

Narrator: Dupin really wore the glasses so that his eyes could search the room without Minister D. suspecting. It did not take long for Dupin to find what he was looking for. His eyes soon fell on a cheap card rack which dangled from a dirty blue ribbon beneath the fireplace mantel. In the rack, plain to see, was a letter. Unlike the purloined letter, it was dirty and crumpled, with a woman's handwriting on the outside.

Dupin: Thank you for seeing me, sir. I have enjoyed our chat.

Minister D.: So have I. Please feel free to call again.

Narrator: Dupin left the room.

Minister D.: Dupin! Wait! *(Dupin is gone.)* The fool. He left his snuff box behind!

Scene Six

Narrator: The next day, Dupin returned to the rooms of Minister D.

Dupin: I'm sorry to trouble you, my friend. I forgot something yesterday.

Minister D.: Your snuff box. Here it is — what is that?!

Narrator: A sound like gunfire cracked through the air, followed by screams. Minister D. rushed to the window. As Minister D. looked out the window, Dupin walked over to the mantle, took the ragged letter from the rack, and replaced it with an exact duplicate he had made.

Minister D. *(turning from the window)*: It is nothing. Some prankster burst a balloon. Well Dupin, will you stay to chat?

Dupin: I am afraid not, my friend. I have what I came for!

Scene Seven

Narrator: Dupin smiled with satisfaction as he told me his story.

Dupin: Of course, the "prankster" with the balloon was an agent I had hired to distract the Minister.

Edgar: But the letter you took looked nothing like the Queen's letter. Hers was neat and addressed in a man's hand. The letter in the rack was ragged, covered with dirt, and addressed by a woman.

Dupin: Of course. It was so unlike the Queen's letter — in every detail — that I knew it must be a fake. When I got it back here, I found the Queen's letter wrapped up inside the false letter.

Edgar: Does Minister D. know he has been had?

Dupin: I doubt it. The copy I made of his letter is perfect. He has no reason to open it up — not until the Queen defies him. When that happens, he is in for a rude surprise.

Edgar: Oh, yes? What did you say in the letter you left?

Dupin: Oh, just a personal message. Something along the lines that scoundrels can hide in plain sight — but not forever!

Edgar Allan Poe...

..."master of the macabre" and the inventor of the detective story, was born on January 19, 1809, in Boston. His parents were actors, and young Edgar was educated in Richmond, Virginia, and schools in England, where his parents lived between 1815-1820. Poe attended the University of Virginia for one year before dropping out in 1825. His first book, a collection of poetry, was published anonymously in 1827. The next year, Poe enrolled as a cadet at West Point.

After leaving West Point, Poe moved in with his aunt Maria Clemm in Richmond, Virginia. In 1832 he won a $50 prize for his short story "MS. Found in a Bottle." Poe became editor of *The Southern Literary Messenger*, and shortly thereafter married his 13-year-old cousin, Virginia Clemm.

In 1841 Poe wrote "The Murders in the Rue Morgue," the world's first detective story. Among his other masterpieces are "The Purloined Letter," "Fall of the House of Usher," and poems *The Raven*, *The Bells*, and *Annabelle Lee*. In 1847 Poe's wife died of tuberculosis. Poe himself died, penniless

FURTHER READING

Students eager to read Poe's other mystery stories should check out "The Murders in the Rue Morgue" and "The Gold Bug."

Of course, Poe's horror stories are unmatched for intensity of emotion and imagery. His first-person crime story "The Tell-Tale Heart" is a brilliant exploration of a criminal's mind. "The Imp of the Perverse" describes in terrifying detail how "ratiocination" — the logic and reasoning employed by Poe's detective Dupin — can lead to madness if not tempered by common sense and honest emotion.

ACTIVITIES

Hide-Away

The key to this mystery story is understanding that the simplest hiding place is often the best hiding place. The official police assume that the letter must be hidden in a well-concealed spot, and spend so much energy looking for a secret hiding place that they ignore the letter hanging in plain sight.

Allow students to play a version of "hide and seek" inspired by this story. Have the students work in pairs. One student picks a hiding place for a "purloined letter" in your classroom and writes it down, concealing it from his or her partner. The other student then asks twenty questions in an attempt to identify the hiding place. Then, have students reverse roles. After each pair has played the game twice, hold a class discussion on which hiding places were easiest to guess and which ones were hardest.

Touch of the Poet

"Perhaps he is not a fool, but then he's a poet, which is almost the same thing..."

Besides inventing the detective story, Edgar Allan Poe also wrote poetry. Have students read one of Poe's narrative poems, such as *The Raven* or *Annabelle Lee*. Assign students to write a short story or play which retells the story Poe told in verse. Advanced students may write a poem of their own which retells the mystery of "The Purloined Letter" or some other story they know well.

My Mystery

"The Purloined Letter," written more than a century ago, centers on a stolen letter. Have students write a contemporary mystery story which centers on modern communication, such as:

◆ an overheard telephone conversation
◆ e-mail sent to the wrong e-mail address
◆ a stolen telephone answering machine tape
◆ a beeper flashing a mysterious telephone number

Poe (continued)
and alone, in a Baltimore tavern on October 7, 1849.

Poe's short life is a tale of personal tragedy and artistic triumph. His writing directly influenced writers as diverse as Dostoevsky, Arthur Conan Doyle, and the poet Rimbaud. He single-handedly invented the modern mystery and horror genres, and is generally considered one of America's greatest poets.

SILVER BLAZE

By Sir Arthur Conan Doyle

Introduction

"Elementary, my dear Watson." Sherlock Holmes, the character who spoke those famous words, is one of the best-known characters in English literature. He's so famous that many people believe Holmes was a real person, and not just a character in books!

This story, "Silver Blaze," is one of Holmes's most baffling mysteries. The author of the story, Sir Arthur Conan Doyle, bet his own wife that she could not figure out the killer's identity. Doyle won the bet with his wife. Now it's your turn to take the challenge. See if you can outsmart Sherlock Holmes, "the world's greatest detective."

Characters

Narrator, *the narrator is Dr. Watson, who looks back on the events in the story*

Sherlock Holmes, *the world's greatest detective*

Dr. John Watson, *Holmes's friend and biographer*

Fitzroy Simpson, *a young gambler*

Edith Baxter, *a housemaid*

Ned Hunter, *a stable boy*

John Straker*, a horse trainer*

Mrs. Straker*, John Straker's wife*

Inspector Gregory, *a detective on the police force*

Colonel Ross, *the wealthy owner of Silver Blaze*

Silas Brown, *a mean old man, and Ross's chief rival*

Boy, *another stable boy*

Scene One

Narrator: It was being called the greatest mystery of the decade — perhaps the century. For days, the newspapers were filled with the strange case of Silver Blaze, the missing racehorse, and John Straker, his murdered trainer. But Sherlock Holmes did not read the newspapers in the days following the crime. He spent his time rambling about our rooms, his chin upon his chest and his brows knitted, puffing away on his pipe. Still, I was not surprised when he announced at breakfast one morning —

Holmes: I am afraid, Watson, that I shall have to go.

Watson: Go! Where to?

Holmes: To Dartmoor.

Watson: Of course! Dartmoor is where Silver Blaze disappeared. My only wonder is that you have not already been mixed up in this extraordinary case.

Holmes: Then you know something about it?

Watson: Certainly. It has been reported in all of the newspapers. I would like to go with you, if I may.

Holmes: My dear Watson, you would do me a great favor by coming. We just have time to catch the train to Dartmoor. I will give you more details on the matter during our journey.

Narrator: And so, an hour later I found myself on a train speeding for Dartmoor with Sherlock Holmes.

Scene Two

Holmes: This is a singular case we are undertaking, Watson.

Watson: I have read all about it in the newspapers. Every issue carries a new story about the mysterious disappearance of Silver Blaze and the murder of his trainer.

Holmes: Yes. But most of those stories have nothing to do with the facts of the case. My challenge is to separate the facts from the mere theories of the police and newspaper reporters.

Watson: And do you have a grip on the facts of the case?

Holmes: I believe I do. Silver Blaze, who belongs to Colonel Ross, is the greatest racehorse in all of England. The horse was entered to run in the race for the Wessex Cup next week. He was the favorite in that race. Enormous sums of money were bet on him.

Watson: That means anyone who bet against Silver Blaze would have a motive for seeing to it that he did not win the race.

Holmes: Exactly. Silver Blaze was kept at Colonel Ross's stable on the moors in Dartmoor. The stable is miles from the nearest village, and the moors around it are a complete wilderness. The stable was run by the horse trainer John Straker, who lived with his wife in a small house a few hundred yards away.

Watson: How long had Straker worked for Colonel Ross?

Holmes: Over 12 years. He has always shown himself to be an honest man.

Watson: I see. Did anyone else live with the Strakers?

Holmes: Three stable boys help take care of the horses. One of these lads sat up all night to guard the horses, while the others slept in the loft. All three were trustworthy lads. The only other person living there was the housemaid, Edith Baxter. She, too, seems to be an honest person.

Watson: So the people working at the stable are not suspects. What exactly happened that fateful night?

Holmes: The horses were exercised and watered as usual, and the stables locked up at nine o'clock. Two of the stable boys went to the house for supper, and the third, Ned Hunter, remained on guard. A few minutes after nine, the maid, Edith Baxter, took Hunter his supper. She was almost to the stables, when a man named Fitzroy Simpson stepped from the shadows. . .

Scene Three

Simpson: Can you tell me where I am?

Baxter *(startled)***:** These are Colonel Ross's training stables.

Simpson: Oh, indeed! What a stroke of luck! I understand that a stable boy keeps watch there all alone at night. Perhaps that is his supper you are taking to him.

Baxter *(nervous)***:** It-it is, sir.

Simpson: How would you like to earn some money? *(He offers her a slip of paper.)* Just give the stable boy this.

Baxter: No-no, sir. Thank you, sir! *(She runs into the stables.)* Ned! Look sharp! A strange man has been asking about you!

Simpson *(appearing at the door)***:** Good evening! I want a word with you, young man.

Hunter *(suspicious)***:** Oh? And what business do you have here?

Simpson: It's business that might put some money in your pocket. Rumor has it that Silver Blaze is not as fast as he once was, and that your bosses are betting against him. Is that true?

Hunter *(angry)***:** So you're a gambler, are you? I'll show you how we handle the likes of you at this stable!

Scene Four

Holmes: With that, Hunter ran to unleash the guard dog to chase away Simpson. The maid turned and ran back to the house — but as she left, she saw Simpson leaning over Hunter's food. By the time Hunter had unleashed the dog, Simpson was gone. Later that night, John Straker was unable to sleep . . .

Mrs. Straker *(sleepy)***:** John? What's the matter?

Straker: You heard what happened at the stables tonight. I'm nervous about Silver Blaze. I'm going to see if he is all right.

Mrs. Straker: But it's almost two o'clock in the morning! And it's raining outside. Don't go, John.

Straker: Don't worry, dear. I'll be right back.

Holmes: But John Straker never returned to his wife. The next morning, Ned Hunter was found passed out — someone had drugged his supper. Silver Blaze was missing from the stable. When the other stable boys searched for the missing horse, they found instead the body of their boss, John Straker. He was lying on the moors hundreds of yards from the stable, his skull crushed. He held in one hand a knife, and in the other he carried a scarf belonging to Fitzroy Simpson. And Silver Blaze was gone!

Scene Five

Narrator: It was evening before Holmes and I reached Tavistock, a little town near the scene of the crime. We were greeted there by Colonel Ross and Inspector Gregory, the police detective in charge of the investigation. The four of us got into a horse-drawn cab and soon were rattling through the streets on our way to Straker's house.

Gregory: The net is drawn pretty close about Fitzroy Simpson. We have already arrested him for the murder of Straker.

Holmes: On what evidence?

Gregory: First, he had bet heavily against Silver Blaze, which gave him the motive to steal the horse. He had the opportunity to poison the stable-boy's food. When we found him the day after the crime his clothes were soaked, so he had certainly been out in the rain. He also owns a heavy walking stick, which could be the murder weapon. Finally, Straker held Simpson's scarf in his hand. The evidence is overwhelming.

Holmes (*shaking his head*)**:** A clever lawyer would tear your case to shreds. First, why would Simpson kidnap the horse? If he wanted to put Silver Blaze out of the race, he would have injured it in the stable. How did he get into the stable after it had been locked for the night? Above all, what did he do with the horse? You still have not found Silver Blaze, have you?

Gregory: No. But that proves nothing. Silver Blaze could be lying dead at the bottom of a bog on the moor. I say that Fitzroy Simpson drugged the stable boy on guard, broke into the stable and kidnapped Silver Blaze. He was making his escape when Straker surprised him. In the struggle that followed, Simpson killed Straker with his stick, then took the horse somewhere and killed it, too.

Holmes: Hmmm. Perhaps you are right. Colonel Ross, are there any other stables nearby?

Ross: Indeed there are. My rival Silas Brown has a stable a few miles across the moor. He, too, has a horse running for the Wessex Cup.

Gregory: We have already inspected Brown's stables, and found no trace of Silver Blaze.

Narrator: With that, Sherlock Holmes fell silent. He seemed lost in thought as our cab approached the lonely Straker house.

Scene Six

Narrator: We all left the cab after it stopped in front of the house. All of us except for Holmes, that is. He sat in the cab with a dreamy expression on his face. When I touched his arm Holmes jumped with a start.

Holmes: Excuse me! I was daydreaming.

Narrator: There was a gleam in his eye which told me that Holmes had his hand upon a clue, though I could not imagine where he had found it.

Gregory: Would you like to visit the scene of the crime, Mr. Holmes?

Holmes: I should prefer to stay here a little. I presume you made an inventory of the things in Straker's pockets at the time of his death, Inspector?

Gregory: The things are in the house, if you would like to see them.

Narrator: Gregory led us into the house, where he showed us a pile of objects on a table. There was a box of matches, a two-inch candle, a pipe and tobacco, some coins, a few papers, and a small, delicate knife.

Holmes (*examining the knife*)**:** This is a singular knife. Watson, this is surely in your line.

Watson: Indeed. It's a doctor's scalpel.

Holmes: A delicate knife for delicate work. A strange weapon for a man to carry.

Gregory: Mrs. Straker says the knife had lain for some days upon the dressing-table, and that Straker picked it up as he left the room. It was a poor weapon, but the best he could lay his hands on at the moment.

Holmes: Very possibly. What are these papers Straker carried with him?

Gregory: Two of them are receipts from a hay-dealer. One of them is a bill from a dress-maker in London for the amount of 37 pounds. It was addressed to William Darbyshire. Mrs. Straker says that Darbyshire was a friend of her husband's, and his mail was sometimes delivered here.

Holmes (*inspecting the bill*)**:** Well, well, well. Mrs. Darbyshire has very expensive tastes! Come, let us visit the scene of the crime.

Narrator: A short walk across the moor took us to the hollow in which the body had been found.

Gregory (*pointing*)**:** We found Straker in the bottom of the hollow. His coat was hanging upon that bush.

Holmes: There was no wind that night, I understand. The coat was not blown against the bush, it was placed there.

Gregory: Yes, it was laid across the bush.

Holmes: You fill me with interest. Now I will take a closer look at things.

Narrator: Holmes got on his hands and knees to inspect the muddy ground in the hollow.

Gregory: We have carefully gone over the ground. I doubt there is anything else to find . . .

Holmes: Halloa! What's this?

Narrator: Holmes held up a mud-covered match.

Gregory (blushing)**:** I can't think how I came to overlook it.

Holmes: It was invisible, buried in the mud. I only saw it because I was looking for it.

Gregory: What! You expected to find it?

Holmes: I thought it not unlikely. Now I would like to take a little walk over the moors before it grows dark.

Ross (scowling)**:** A walk? With my trainer murdered and my horse missing? (to Gregory) Come back to the house with me, Inspector. I need your advice. Should I officially remove Silver Blaze from the coming race?

Holmes: Certainly not! Silver Blaze will be in that race!

Ross: I am very glad to have your opinion, sir. I would much rather have my horse!

Scene Seven

Narrator: Holmes and I slowly walked across the moor. The sun was setting behind the distant buildings of Silas Brown's stables. But the beauty of the landscape was lost on my companion, who was sunk in the deepest thought.

Holmes: We may leave for the moment the question of who killed John Straker. Let us concentrate on what happened to the horse. Now, supposing he broke away during or after the murder, where would he have gone? A horse is a gregarious animal — it wants to be with other horses. He would either return to Colonel Ross's stables, or he would head for Silas Brown's stables. Since Silver Blaze is not at Ross's stable, he must be at Silas Brown's.

Narrator: Soon we came to the gates at Brown's stable. A fierce-looking elderly man strode through the gate with a hunting crop swinging from his hand.

Brown: What's this? What the devil do you want here?

Holmes (sweetly)**:** Ten minutes talk with you, my good sir.

Brown: I've no time to talk to every gadabout. We want no strangers here. Be off, or you will find a dog at your heels!

Narrator: Holmes leaned forward and whispered something in Brown's ears. The man started violently and flushed to the temples.

Brown: It's a lie! An infernal lie!

Holmes: Very good! Should we argue about it here, in public, or talk it over in your home?

Brown: Oh, come in if you wish to.

Narrator: Holmes followed Brown into the house. When they returned twenty minutes later, Brown's bullying manner was gone. He cringed along at Holmes's side like a dog with its master.

Brown: Your instructions will be done. It shall be done!

Holmes (*threatening*)**:** There must be no mistake!

Brown (*wincing*)**:** Oh, no. There shall be no mistake! You can trust me! You can trust me!

Narrator: With that, Holmes and I began the walk back to Ross's stable.

Holmes: I have never met a more perfect compound of the bully, coward, and sneak than Mr. Silas Brown.

Watson: He has Silver Blaze, then?

Holmes: He tried to bluster his way out of it. But I described his exact actions to him — how he saw the strange horse wandering on the moor. How he was shocked to discover it was Silver Blaze, his main competition for the coming race. And how he had sneaked Silver Blaze into his own stables and painted over the horse's white markings so that the police would never recognize the animal. Now Brown is convinced I was watching, and saw the whole thing!

Watson: Aren't you afraid to leave the horse with him?

Holmes: My dear Watson, he will guard it like the apple of his eye. Brown knows his only hope of mercy is to produce it safe.

Watson: Colonel Ross will be pleased to hear that his horse is found.

Holmes: Hmmm. Perhaps you noticed that Colonel Ross has been a trifle disrespectful of me. I would like to have a little fun at his expense. Say nothing to him about the horse.

Watson: Certainly not — not without your permission.

Holmes: And, of course, the matter of the horse is minor compared with the question of who killed John Straker.

Watson: And you will devote yourself to that?

Holmes: On the contrary. We will return to London by the night train.

Scene Eight

Narrator: I was thunderstruck by my friend's words. I could not understand why he would abandon an investigation that had begun so brilliantly. Not a word more would he say as we headed back to Straker's house. It was dark by the time we joined Colonel Ross and Inspector Gregory there.

Holmes: Watson and I return to London by the midnight train.

Ross *(sneering)*: So, you don't think you can arrest the murderer of poor Straker?

Holmes *(shrugging)*: There are certain difficulties in the way. Inspector Gregory, do you have a photograph of John Straker?

Gregory *(handing Holmes an envelope)*: Right here.

Holmes: Excellent!

Narrator: As we left the house, Holmes glanced over at a nearby pen which held a dozen or so sheep. A stable boy stood at the pen. A sudden idea seemed to strike Holmes.

Holmes *(calling)*: Boy! Have you noticed anything wrong with the sheep lately?

Boy: Not really, sir. But three of them have gone lame.

Holmes *(chuckling)*: A long shot, Watson. A very long shot!

Gregory *(confused)*: You think the fact that the sheep have become lame is important?

Holmes: Very much so.

Gregory: Is there any other point that you think is important?

Holmes: Yes. The curious behavior of the guard dog on the night Silver Blaze was kidnapped.

Gregory: But the dog didn't do anything!

Holmes: That was the curious behavior.

Stop!
Match wits with Sherlock Holmes!
Holmes has uncovered all of the clues you need to solve the mystery of Silver Blaze.

◆ Who kidnapped Silver Blaze?
◆ Who killed John Straker?
◆ What exactly happened that fateful night?

Do you have the answers? Then read on to see if you are right!

~~~~~~~~~~~~~~~~~~~~~~~~~~~~~~~~

Scene Nine

Narrator: Four days later, Holmes and I were again on the train to Dartmoor. We were off to see the race for the Wessex Cup. Colonel Ross met us at the train, and drove us to the racetrack.

Ross: I have seen nothing of my horse.

Holmes: I suppose you would know him if you saw him?

Ross *(angry)*: I have owned racehorses for 20 years, and was never asked such a stupid question! A child would recognize Silver Blaze with his white forehead!

Narrator: Holmes, Colonel Ross, and I arrived at the track. The Colonel was surprised to see a horse take his place at the starting gate. He was even more shocked when the horse easily won the race! We went to the track and joined the winning horse and jockey.

Ross: Is it — could it be Silver Blaze?

Holmes: You have only to wash his face and you will see the same Silver Blaze as ever. I found him in the hands of a faker and took the liberty of having him sent over in time for the race.

Ross: My dear sir, you have done wonders. I owe you a thousand apologies. You have done me a great service by finding my horse. You would do me a greater service by finding the murderer of poor John Straker.

Holmes *(quietly)*: I have done so.

Ross: You have got him? Where is he?

Holmes: He is here.

Ross: Here! Where?

Holmes: In my company at the present moment.

Ross *(angry)*: What? You suspect me?!

Holmes *(laughing)*: Of course not, Colonel. The real murderer is standing just behind you.

Narrator: With that, Holmes placed his hand upon the glossy neck of Silver Blaze.

Ross and Watson: The horse!

Holmes: Yes, the horse. And might I add that it was in self-defense, and that Mr. John Straker was not a trustworthy man!

Scene Ten

Narrator: Holmes, Colonel Ross, and I had a train car to ourselves on the trip back to London. During the journey Holmes explained how he had unraveled the mystery.

Holmes: I must confess that at first I agreed with Inspector Gregory. It seemed likely that Fitzroy Simpson was the culprit, but I knew that the case was far from complete. It was when I learned that Silas Brown's stable was so close at hand that I began to consider other solutions to the crime. Then, when I saw what Straker was carrying when he was murdered, I grew convinced that there was more to the case than met the eye.

Ross: What raised your suspicions?

Holmes: The first thing was the knife Straker carried that night. As Watson pointed out, it was a knife used by doctors — not a weapon. It struck me that it was just the sort of knife a man would carry if he were planning to knick the back of a horse's leg, thus making it lame.

Ross: Villain! Scoundrel!

Holmes: When I saw that Straker carried another man's bills in his pockets, I grew even more suspicious. As a man of the world, Colonel, you know that men do not carry other men's bills. It seemed likely to me that Straker was leading a double-life, and keeping a second household in London. This provided a financial motivation for his actions. Straker had bet against Silver Blaze, and was about to cripple the animal when it struck him down.

Watson: But exactly what happened that night, Holmes?

Holmes: First, Straker drugged his stable-boy's supper. Then, in the middle of the night, he sneaked down to the stable and led Silver Blaze from its stall. The dog, which knew Straker, did not bark, as it would have done if Fitzroy Simpson had broken in.

Ross: Of course! We have been blind. That's what you meant by the dog's curious behavior.

Holmes: What else could I have meant? As Straker led Silver Blaze out onto the moor, he came across Simpson's scarf, which the unlucky man had dropped earlier. Straker picked it up, possibly thinking he could later use it to bind the horse's wound. When he got to the hollow, Straker removed his coat and placed it on the bush. He then struck a match in order to light his candle. Silver Blaze, frightened at the sudden glare, lashed out. Its metal shoe struck Straker a fatal blow. Do I make it clear?

Ross: Wonderful! You might have been there!

Holmes: My final shot was, I confess, a long one. It struck me that Straker may have practiced before trying to cripple Silver Blaze. When the stable boy told me a few of the sheep had come lame, I was certain of Straker's guilt. The next day I showed his photograph at the dress-maker's shop in London. They told me he was an excellent customer, known to them as Darbyshire, who had a very dashing wife with expensive tastes. I have no doubt this woman plunged Straker over head and ears in debt. That forced him into this desperate plot.

Ross: Excellent work, Mr. Holmes.

Holmes: The case was simple, once I had possession of the facts. We will be in London soon. If you would care to join us at dinner, Colonel Ross, I would be happy to give you any other details of the case which might interest you.

Sir Arthur Conan Doyle...

...is best known for creating Sherlock Holmes, perhaps the most popular character in English literature.

Doyle was born in Edinburgh, Scotland, on May 22, 1859. He attended medical school in Edinburgh, where one of his teachers, a keen-eyed, hawk-nosed doctor named John Bell, amazed his students with his amazing ability to deduce facts from seemingly random clues.

In 1887, Doyle, who was a practicing physician in London, published a short novel, *A Study in Scarlet*, featuring Sherlock Holmes and his sidekick, Dr. Watson. (Holmes was modeled on Doyle's old teacher, Dr. Bell.) It would be another three years before Doyle would publish *The Sign of Four*, the second mystery story starring Holmes. Soon, though, Holmes became a phenomenon throughout the English-speaking world.

Starting in 1890, a new magazine, *The Strand*, published a series of short stories starring Holmes and Watson. The duo caught the public imagination. Soon, Doyle had abandoned his medical practice altogether and was writing full-time. "Silver Blaze," written 1892, was

FURTHER READING

Students who enjoyed this story are in for a treat — the 56 short stories and four novels featuring Sherlock Holmes that Doyle wrote in his career! Holmes was perhaps at his best in the first two collections of stories — *The Adventures of Sherlock Holmes* and *The Memoirs of Sherlock Holmes*. The novel *The Hound of the Baskervilles* is probably the finest of all Holmes stories.

Readers who enjoy Holmes may also like to meet his counterpart — Raffles. This character, a reformed thief who uses his skills for good, stars in a series of stories written by E.W. Hornung.

Fans looking for more puzzling British mysteries will enjoy the Father Brown short stories by G.K. Chesterton.

ACTIVITIES
Unusual Suspect

As he was writing "Silver Blaze," Arthur Conan Doyle bet his wife that she would not guess the killer's identity. He won his bet!

Ask students if they suspected the horse as the killer. Then have them go back and pick out the clues pointing to the true solution of the crime (such as the dog not barking as Silver Blaze was stolen from the stable, the scalpel in Straker's hand, the match buried in the mud, Straker's coat draped across the bush, and so on).

Tell students to imagine that Sherlock Holmes had not been around to solve the case. Challenge them to describe a "solution" to the case naming either Fitzroy Simpson or Silas Brown as the killer. Tell them their solutions must take into account all of the clues pointing to the killer. Discuss how ingeniously Conan Doyle structured the story, leaving only one possible solution that still comes as a complete surprise to the reader.

Extra! Extra!

"For days, the newspapers were filled with the strange case of Silver Blaze..."

Newspapers in Victorian England were known for their sensational reports of crimes. They were very similar to today's "tabloid TV" programs and supermarket-checkout magazines.

Have students pretend that they are newspaper reporters covering the Silver Blaze case, and their assignment is to write a newspaper account of Sherlock Holmes's solution of the mystery. Point out that their challenge is to attract as many readers as possible. What headline will they use? How will they open the story? What quotes will they use?

My Mystery

One hundred years ago, horse racing was one of the most popular sports in England, and the race described in the story would be the equivalent of the Super Bowl or World Series today.

Let students write their own contemporary sports mystery story. They may wish to feature elements such as:

◆ a star athlete is missing before a big game

◆ a coach is accused of "throwing" a game

◆ a referee or umpire is bribed to favor one
   team over another

Doyle (continued)
the first story in the second collection of Holmes' stories, *The Memoirs of Sherlock Holmes*.

By 1893, Doyle had grown tired of Holmes and "killed off" the great detective in the story "The Final Problem." Fortunately for mystery-lovers, though, Doyle resurrected his hero in 1902 with *The Hound of the Baskervilles*. Doyle continued to write stories about Holmes and Watson until he died in 1930.

Sir Arthur Conan Doyle, in addition to creating Sherlock Holmes, wrote historical fiction and science fiction stories. In fact, with *The Lost World*, Doyle invented the stock science fiction convention of modern men encountering dinosaurs. Michael Crichton, another physician-turned-author, used both the premise and the title in his own work.

THE ETHICS OF PIG

By O. Henry

Introduction

"Con man" is short for "confidence man." He makes his living in a simple, dishonest way — he wins your confidence, takes your money, and then leaves you behind.

"The Ethics of Pig" is about a con man who finds a partner to help him work his con. As you read the play, see if you can tell who's the real con man in the pair.

Characters

Jefferson Peters, *a con artist*

Rufe Tatum, *a young man living in the backwoods*

Storekeeper,
Sheriff } *two people from Rufe's hometown*

George B. Tapley, *a circus manager*

Mac, *a circus worker*

Ad Man, *a newspaper worker*

Narrator, *the narrator is Jefferson Peters, looking back at what happens in the play*

Scene One

Narrator: I'm not afraid to admit how I earn a living. I am in the line of "unlegal graft." That is to say, I'm a con artist. Don't think I take money from widows or orphans or other poor folks. No, I take advantage of people with a few bucks to spend who are looking to get rich quick. Now, in my line of business, the hardest thing is to find an upright and trustworthy partner to work a swindle with. So, last summer, I decided to head into the backwoods country to see if I could find a partner naturally gifted with a talent for crime, but not yet spoiled by success. . . .

Scene Two

Narrator: I found a tiny village that seemed like a good place to find a partner. I headed down to the general store, where the town sages gathered.

Peters: Gentlemen, I don't suppose there is another community in the whole world in which crime and wrongdoing are more rare than here.

Storekeeper: Why, thank you, sir. I reckon we air about as moral a community as there be, according to censuses of opinion. But I reckon you ain't ever met Rufe Tatum.

Sheriff: Why no, he can't hardly have ever. That Rufe is shore the biggest scalawag that has ever escaped hanging. That reminds me — I ought to have let Rufe out of jail the day before yesterday. The thirty days he got for stealing Yance Goodloe's pig was up then. Oh, well. A day or two more behind bars won't hurt Rufe any.

Narrator: I decided to get to know this Rufe Tatum.

Scene Three

Narrator: A few days after Rufe got out of jail, he and I sat down for a little talk. What I needed in a partner was someone who looked honest. Rufe was perfect for the part. He was about the size of a first baseman, with blue eyes and wavy hair the color of a sunset over the Grand Canyon. He looked like the perfect rube. I told Rufe about my line of work, and that I was looking for a partner. He was ready to jump at the job.

Peters: So you're interested in helping me?

Rufe: I shore am.

Peters: What have you done that qualifies you for the job?

Rufe: Why, ain't you heard tell? There ain't another man in the county that can tote off a pig as easy as I without being heard, seen, or catched.

Peters: You don't say?

Rufe: I can grab a pig from under a porch, at the trough, in the woods, day or night, any-where or anyhow, and I guarantee nobody won't hear a squeal. It's all in the way you grab them, y'see.

Peters: That's very impressive —

Rufe: Why, I hope one day to be rekernized as the champion pig-stealer of the world!

Peters: It's good to have a goal. And hog-stealing is a fine line of work — in this town. But there is a lot more to be had in this world than a handful of pigs. I have one thousand dollars cash capital. With that money, and your down-home looks, I think we can take a few dollars from the suckers of the world.

Rufe: Well, golly. I'm your man!

Narrator: I sealed our partnership by shaking his huge hog-stealing hand.

Scene Four

Narrator: Rufe and I left town, and over the next few weeks I trained him for his part in the shell game. Rufe would be the "innocent bystander" who won money from me. Then the suckers watching would join the game. Before you knew it, we'd have all of their excess cash. Rufe and I headed for the midwest, and got as far as Lexington. The Binkley Brothers Circus was in town there! Now, the circus is the perfect place to run the shell game. So Rufe and I got rooms in a boarding house, and agreed to meet that afternoon at the circus. Late that night. . . .

Peters: What is that racket? It sounds like it's coming from Rufe's room.

Narrator: I headed down the hall. Rufe was awake in his room, pouring some milk into a tin pan for a dingy-white, half-grown, squealing pig.

Peters: Where were you today, Rufe? We were supposed to meet outside the circus.

Rufe: Now don't be hard on me, Mr. Peters. You know how long I been stealing pigs. It's got to be a habit with me, I guess. I was waiting for you at that circus, when I just couldn't pass up the chance to steal this here little feller.

Peters: Well, maybe you've got klepto-pig-ia. But why would you waste your time with this runt?

Rufe: Why, Mr. Peters, you just don't understand pigs they way I do. This here seems to me to be an animal of real intelligence. He walked half way across the room on his hind legs just a while ago.

Peters: Wonderful. I'm going back to bed now. See if you can persuade your intelligent new friend to keep quiet!

Scene Five

Narrator: I always read the morning newspaper when I'm working a town. The next morning, I almost choked on my coffee as I looked at the paper. There was an ad, printed smack dab on the front page.

Peters (*reading*)**:** "Five Thousand Dollar Reward! This amount will be paid, and no questions asked, for the return, alive and unharmed, of Beppo, the famous European educated pig, that strayed or was stolen from the side-show tents of Binkley Brothers circus yesterday. Signed, George B. Tapley, Business Manager."

Narrator: I folded up the paper and slipped it in my pocket and went to Rufe's room. He was feeding the pig some milk and apple peelings.

Peters: Well, well, well. Good morning, all. So we are up? And piggy is having his breakfast. Er, what are you planning to do with that pig, Rufe?

Rufe: I'm going to crate him up and ship him back home to Ma. He'll be company for her while I'm away.

Peters: He's a mighty fine pig.

Rufe (*his feelings hurt*)**:** You were calling him names last night.

Peters: Oh, well. He looks better to me this morning. I was raised on a farm, and I'm very fond of pigs. Tell you what I'll do, Rufe. I'll give you ten dollars for that pig.

Rufe: Well. . . . I reckon I won't sell this pig. If it was any other one I might.

Peters: Why not this one?

Rufe: Because stealing it was the grandest achievement of my life. There ain't another man alive that could have done it. It was in a tent, you see, on a platform, tied with this little chain. There was a giant and a lady with a beard in the tent next door. So I snuck in, got the pig and crawled under the canvas of the tent without him squeaking as loud as a mouse. I stuck him under my coat, and brought him back here.

Peters: Very impressive.

Rufe (*blushing with pride*)**:** I reckon I won't ever sell that pig, Mr. Peters. If I ever have grandchildren, I'll sit them around the fire and tell them how their grand-dad stole this here pig.

Peters: The pig won't live that long — your grandchildren will just have to take your word for it. I'll give you one hundred dollars for it.

Rufe (*surprised*)**:** The pig can't be worth that much to you. What do you want him for?

Peters (*thinking fast*)**:** You wouldn't know it to look at me, Rufe, but I have an artistic side. I collect pigs. I have scoured the world for prize pigs. And this pig has the look of a champion, Rufe!

Rufe: I wish I could help you. But I've got an artistic tenement, too. Stealing pigs is my art. Pigs are an inspiration to me — especially this one. I wouldn't sell him, not for two hundred and fifty dollars.

Peters (*wiping sweat from his brow*)**:** Now listen, it's not so much a matter of business with me as art. My pig collection is my gift to the world. It won't be complete without this fine pig of yours. According to the ethics of pig, I offer you five hundred dollars for this animal.

Rufe: Mr. Peters, it ain't the money. It's sentiment. I love this pig.

Peters: Seven hundred dollars

Rufe: Make it eight hundred, and I'll drive the love from my heart.

Peters: Done!

Scene Six

Narrator: I paid Rufe, who said he was going into town to buy some shoes. I put the pig in a sack and hustled down to the circus. I found George B. Tapley in a little tent with a window flap open.

Peters: Well, I've got it!

Tapley: Be specific. Do you have the guinea pigs for the Asiatic python, or the alfalfa for the sacred buffalo?

Peters: Neither. I've got Beppo, the European educated pig, in a sack outside this tent. I found him rooting around in my front yard this morning. I'll take the five thousand in large bills, if it's handy.

Narrator: George B. gave me a funny look, then leaned back to the window flap. A man was feeding carrots to a huge black pig across the way.

Tapley (*calling*)**:** Hey, Mac! Anything wrong with the educated wonder of the world this morning?

Mac: Nope! She's eating like a pig!

Tapley (*to Peters*)**:** Sorry, buddy. You're mistaken. You probably ate too many pork chops last night.

Peters (*showing the newspaper*)**:** But — but look at this ad!

Tapley (*reading the ad*)**:** It's fake. Don't know anything about it. But I do know that Beppo, the marvelous, world-wide porcine wonder of the four-footed world, is enjoying her breakfast right now, unstrayed and unstolen. Good day!

Scene Seven

Narrator: I was beginning to see the light. First, I took the pig in the sack and let it free in a barnyard along with dozens of other squealing little hogs. Then I headed to the newspaper offices, and went to the advertising desk.

Peters: How would you describe the man who placed the ad about Beppo the pig? Was he short, fat, and bald?

Ad Man: Why, no. He was about six feet four and a half inches tall, with pale blue eyes and wavy red hair.

Narrator: That was that. I'd been had by a stealer of hogs. I took the two hundred dollars I had left and headed out of town. . . .What's that you say? My greed did me in? If I had only offered to split the reward with Rufe, I would still have my money? Don't be silly. I just tried to do what any businessman does. Buy low and sell high — isn't that how business works? Stocks, bonds, and pigs . . . what's the difference?

AFTER TWENTY YEARS

By O. Henry

Introduction

Two friends grow up together in the big city. They are like brothers. Then, one of them leaves town and returns twenty years later. Which friend has changed the most — the one who left, or the one who stayed behind?

This mysterious story of friendship and betrayal is as relevant today as when it was written almost 100 years ago.

Characters

Narrator
Bob, *a well-dressed man*
Policeman
Young Bob, *Bob, twenty years before the time in which this play is set*
Young Jimmy, *Young Bob's best friend*
Man

Scene One

Narrator: A New York City policeman on the beat walks up an avenue. The street is empty. The time is almost ten o'clock at night, and chilly gusts of wind with a taste of rain in them blow. The policeman slows in front of a dark doorway. A man named Bob stands in the shadows there.

Bob: It's all right officer. I'm just waiting for friend.

Policeman: Yes?

Bob: It's an appointment made twenty years ago. Sounds a little funny to you, doesn't it? Let me explain. About that long ago there used to be a restaurant where this store stands — Big Joe Brady's restaurant.

Policeman: Until five years ago. It was torn down then.

Narrator: The man in the doorway strikes a match and lights his cigar. The light shows a pale, square-jawed face with keen eyes and a little white scar near his right eyebrow. He wears a large diamond pin in his scarf.

Bob: Twenty years ago tonight I dined here at Big Joe Brady's with Jimmy Wells, my best chum and the finest chap in the world. He and I were raised right here in New York, just like two brothers, together. I was eighteen and Jimmy was twenty . . .

Scene Two

Narrator: Twenty years previously, young Bob and Jimmy talk at Big Joe Brady's restaurant.

Young Bob: Are you sure that you don't want to head west with me, Jimmy? I'm telling you, we can make our fortunes out there.

Young Jimmy: I guess I'll stay right here in New York, Bob. To my mind, this is the only place on earth.

Young Bob: I'll miss you, pal.

Young Jimmy: And I'll miss you.

Young Bob: Say, why don't we make an appointment to meet each other again?

Young Jimmy: What do you mean?

Young Bob: Let's meet up again, years from now, when we'll have our destinies worked out and our fortunes made. What do you say we meet again in twenty years?

Young Jimmy: I get you. A reunion.

Young Bob: Exactly!

Young Jimmy: No matter who we are, or what we're doing, or how far we have to come, twenty years from tonight let's meet right here, at Big Joe Brady's restaurant.

Young Bob: It's a deal. I'll see you then, pal!

Scene Three

Policeman: It sounds pretty interesting. Seems like a long time between meets, though. Haven't you heard from your friend since you left?

Bob: Well, yes. For a time we wrote letters. But after a year or two we lost track of each other. But I know Jimmy will meet me here if he's still alive. He was the truest, staunchest chap that ever lived. He'll never forget. I came a thousand miles to stand in this door tonight, and it's worth it if my old partner turns up!

Narrator: Bob takes a diamond-studded watch from his pocket.

Bob: It's three minutes to ten. It was exactly ten o'clock when we parted here at the restaurant door.

Policeman: Did pretty well in the West, didn't you?

Bob: You bet! I hope Jimmy has done half as well. He was kind of a plodder, though, good fellow that he was. I had to compete with some of the sharpest wits going to get my fortune.

Policeman: I'll be on my way. Hope your friend comes around all right. Are you going to give him until ten o'clock, then head out?

Bob: I should say not! I'll wait for him at least until ten-thirty — maybe longer! So long, officer!

Policeman: Good night, sir!

Scene Four

Narrator: A fine, cold drizzle begins to fall. Bob waits, smoking his cigar. After twenty minutes, a tall man in a light overcoat, its collar turned up to his ears, crosses the street.

Man: Is that you, Bob?

Bob: Is that you, Jimmy Wells?

Man: Bless my heart! It's Bob, sure as fate. I was certain I'd find you here if you were still alive. Well, well, well! The restaurant's gone, Bob. I wish it had lasted, so we could have had another dinner there. How has the West treated you, old man?

Bob: Bully! It has given me everything I asked it for. You've changed lots, Jimmy. I never thought you were so tall.

Man: Oh, I grew a bit after I was twenty.

Bob: Are you doing well here in New York, Jimmy?

Man: Moderately. I work for the city. Come on, Bob, we'll go around to a place I know of, and have a good long talk about old times.

Narrator: The two men walk up the street, arm in arm. Bob, his ego enlarged by success, tells his companion all about his career. The other man listens with interest. Soon they pass a brightly-lit drugstore. In the glare of the lights, the two men take a good look at each other.

Bob: Hold on! You're not Jimmy Wells! Twenty years is a long time, but it's not long enough to turn a man's eyes from brown to blue!

Man: It can be long enough time to turn a good man into a bad one. You've been under arrest for the past ten minutes, "Silky" Bob. The Chicago police department thought you might be heading our way. They sent us a telegram saying they wanted a little chat with you.

Bob (*sighs*): I'll come quietly. But how did you know where to find me?

Man: Here's a note I was asked to hand to you. You can read it before I take you to the station. It's from Patrolman Wells.

Narrator: Bob reads the note.

Policeman: Dear Bob, I was at the appointed place on time. When you struck the match to light your cigar, I recognized your face from a "wanted" poster sent from Chicago. Somehow I couldn't arrest you myself, so I went around and got a plain clothes detective to do the job. Signed, your friend after twenty years, Jimmy.

O. Henry...

...was born William Sydney Porter in Greensboro, North Carolina, on September 11, 1862, and lived a life with as many twists as any of his stories. Porter, raised by his grandmother, attended a small school run by his aunt. As a young man, he moved west and settled in Austin, Texas. There, he worked on a ranch before finding a job as a bank teller. While in Austin, Porter married and published his own newspaper, *The Rolling Stone*.

By 1896, however, Porter's life was shattered. His wife had contracted tuberculosis, *The Rolling Stone* was failing, and Porter himself was accused of stealing from the bank where he worked. Porter fled the country for Honduras, only to return six months later to visit his dying wife. Porter was arrested and convicted of embezzlement. While serving time in prison, Porter began writing fiction and assumed the pen name O. Henry.

Released from prison in 1901, Porter moved to New York City. He soon was hired by the *New York World*, which assigned him to write a

FURTHER READING

O. Henry left behind dozens of entertaining stories to appeal to readers of all ages. His best-known stories include the hilarious "Ransom of Red Chief" and the uplifting "A Retrieved Reformation."

Readers who enjoy the Ellery Queen play in this book, "As Simple as ABC," will also want to check out O. Henry's story "Two Renegades," which uses a twist similar to the Queen mystery.

ACTIVITIES

THE ETHICS OF PIG
A Con Man on Trial

Peters justifies his criminal acts by saying he only takes advantage of people looking to "get rich quick." Have students stage a mock trial of Peters. Allow two students to be attorneys — one prosecuting Peters for running the shell game, the other defending his actions. After they state their cases, have them cross examine a student playing the role of Peters. Then have the rest of the class deliberate as a jury to find Peters guilty or not guilty of fraud.

Sounds of the South?

One way O. Henry shows the reader that his characters are from the rural south is his use of dialect. That means O. Henry writes the dialogue as the characters would actually speak, not in proper English. Here is one of Rufe's lines:

> *"Why, ain't you heard tell? There ain't another man in the county that can tote off a pig as easy as I without being heard, seen, or catched."*

Have students "translate" the line into proper English. Then ask them to rewrite other lines from the play written in dialect as proper English. Finally, have them pick lines written in proper English and rewrite them as they would have been spoken by Rufe or his small-town neighbors.

My Mystery

The twist to "The Ethics of Pig" is a classic reversal — the character assumed to be a slow-witted rube outsmarts the professional con-man.

Have students write their own story with twist. It may be set anywhere and at anytime, but the final twist must be a reversal in which one character turns the tables on another. Possible situations could include:

- ◆ a grandparent who turns out to be a whiz at video games
- ◆ a small kid who is a champion basketball player
- ◆ a shy, quiet kid whose parent is a movie star

AFTER TWENTY YEARS

A Friend Indeed?

The plot in which one friend becomes a criminal while another joins the police has been used time and again in mystery stories and movies. In this story, policeman Jimmy Wells has his old friend "Silky" Bob arrested. Jimmy faced an ethical dilemma — whether to be loyal to his job as a police officer or to be loyal to his old friend.

Ask students what they would have done if they had been in Jimmy's shoes. Have them list the other possible options Jimmy might have chosen, such as telling Bob that he would be arrested unless he changed his ways, warning Bob that he was wanted and allowing him to go free, or not doing anything at all. Have students discuss whether or not they believe Jimmy did the right thing, and have them give reasons for their beliefs.

Wanted!

Jimmy recognizes his friend from a wanted poster. Point out that this story was written before photographs were easily reproduced, and that wanted posters often carried written descriptions of people. Have students write "wanted" posters for themselves or a favorite celebrity. Tell students that the "crimes" are not important, but accurate descriptions are! The posters should describe the person's appearance, unique characteristics, names and nicknames, and any other important information.

My Mystery

Ask students to imagine that they are going to move away at the end of the school year, and will not see their classmates until they meet for a class reunion in 20 years. Have students write mystery stories or plays set at that reunion in which they clear up a mystery that occurred sometime in the past.

Henry (continued) short story each week for the newspaper's Sunday edition. Over the next nine years, Porter turned out the short, ironic stories that have made him one of the most well-read authors in history.

Unfortunately, Porter's personal life remained unhappy. "O. Henry," whose stories are still read and loved, died a penniless alcoholic on June 5, 1910.

THE SEVEN CREAM JUGS

By Saki

Characters

Mr. Pigeoncote, *a wealthy British man, celebrating his twenty-fifth wedding anniversary*

Mrs. Pigeoncote, *wife of Mr. Pigeoncote*

Wilfrid, *their cousin*

Mrs. Consuelo Von Bullyon, *a house guest*

Narrator

Scene One

Narrator: The Pigeoncotes, Peter and his wife, sit in their comfortable home in London. They have recently celebrated their twenty-fifth wedding anniversary. They are tired of counting all of the silver presents sent to them by family and friends, and are sharing family gossip.

Mrs. Pigeoncote: I suppose young Wilfrid Pigeoncote will never visit us, now that he has inherited all of that money.

Mr. Pigeoncote: Well, we can hardly expect him to, seeing that we snubbed him when he was a nobody. I don't think I've set eyes on him since he was a boy of twelve.

Mrs. Pigeoncote: There was a good reason we never encouraged him to visit. With that notorious — er — problem of his, Wilfrid was not the sort of person one wanted in one's house.

Mr. Pigeoncote: Well, the "problem" still exists, doesn't it? Or do you think inheriting a fortune will reform the young man?

Mrs. Pigeoncote: Of course not. But the problem doesn't seem as serious now. When a man is wealthy, this sort of thing is no longer considered theft. It becomes instead an interesting personality quirk.

Narrator: The Pigeoncotes are discussing their relative Wilfrid.

Introduction

A kleptomaniac steals anything he can lay his hands on. To people like the Pigeoncotes, the stars of this play, a kleptomaniac is a terrible person — unless he also happens to be rich.

This comic story is about a case of mistaken identity. It shows what happens when you assume you know more than you really do. As you read the play, keep in mind that people are not always whom they appear to be.

Wilfrid, a young man of twenty-five, is known throughout the Pigeoncote family as "Wilfrid the Snatcher." He is a kleptomaniac. When Wilfrid visits, nothing in the house smaller than the dining room table is safe. He will carry off anything, provided it belongs to someone else.

Mr. Pigeoncote (*reading a telegram*)**:** This is funny. Here's a telegram from Wilfrid. He's driving through town in his car, and would like to stop and pay his respects. He asks if he can stay the night.

Mrs. Pigeoncote: Are you sure it's from the Wilfrid? Wilfrid the Snatcher? The name Wilfrid is so common in the family.

Mr. Pigeoncote: It must be from him. None of the other Wilfrids has a car.

Mrs. Pigeoncote (*looking at their gifts*)**:** This is an awkward time to have a person with his problem in the house. We have all of these silver gifts lying around — and more coming every day in the mail. I can hardly keep track of them all as it is.

Mr. Pigeoncote: We must keep a sharp look-out, that's all.

Mrs. Pigeoncote: But these kleptomaniacs are so clever . . . especially when they have been at it as long as Wilfrid!

Scene Two

Narrator: When Wilfrid arrives, the Pigeoncotes treat him kindly — but eye him like a hawk. After dinner, they show Wilfrid their silver anniversary presents.

Mrs. Pigeoncote (*nervous*)**:** They are such useful gifts. There are some duplicates, of course.

Mr. Pigeoncote: For instance, we already have received seven cream jugs.

Mrs. Pigeoncote: Imagine that! We'd have to drink nothing but cream to use them all! Of course, we will exchange some of the duplicates.

Wilfrid: Do you mind if I take a closer look at your gifts?

Mrs. Pigeoncote: Well . . . .

Mr. Pigeoncote (*swallowing hard*)**:** If you must.

Narrator: Wilfrid looks closely at the silver gifts displayed on the table. Mrs. Pigeoncote eyes him like a cat whose newly born kittens are being handed round for inspection.

Mrs. Pigeoncote: Let me see. Where is the silver mustard-pot?

Wilfrid: Sorry. I set it down over there.

Mrs. Pigeoncote: Humph. And where is the sugar pot?

Wilfrid: I put it down over there. Why?

Mrs. Pigeoncote: I — er — I want to label whom it comes from before I forget.

Narrator: Wilfrid eventually says good-night and goes to bed. As soon as he is gone, the Pigeoncotes count their silver gifts.

Mr. Pigeoncote: There's only thirty-four gifts here!

Mrs. Pigeoncote: There should be thirty-five! Right?

Mr. Pigeoncote: I think so. *(suddenly angry)* The cheap young hound didn't bring us a gift — I'll be hanged if he carries one off!

Mrs. Pigeoncote: Tomorrow when he's taking his bath he's sure to leave his keys in his room. We can search his suitcase — it's the only thing to do.

Scene Three

Narrator: The next morning, the Pigeoncotes huddle together in the hall closet, the door opened a crack. They stare at the door of the guest bedroom across the hall. Eventually the door opens and Wilfrid, whistling a happy tune, leaves the room and heads to the bathroom.

Mr. Pigeoncote: Say, that's a nice robe he's wearing.

Mrs. Pigeoncote: Forget his robe! Let's go get our silver!

Narrator: The Pigeoncotes rush into the room and search the dresser for Wilfrid's keys. They find them and unlock Wilfrid's suitcase.

Mrs. Pigeoncote *(in triumph)***:** Ah-ha!

Narrator: She holds up a silver cream jug, which had been tucked in among Wilfrid's clothes.

Mr. Pigeoncote: The cunning brute! He took one of the cream jugs because there were so many of them. He thought we wouldn't miss it.

Mrs. Pigeoncote: Quick! Let's take it down and put it back with the others.

Narrator: Wilfrid is late coming down to breakfast. When he joins the Pigeoncotes at the table, he seems ill-at-ease.

Wilfrid: I have an unpleasant thing to say. I'm afraid that one of your servants must be a thief!

Mrs. Pigeoncote *(shocked)***:** A thief?

Wilfrid: Yes. Something has been taken from my suitcase. It was a little gift for you from my mother and myself

Mr. and Mrs. Pigeoncote: Did you say from your mother?!

Mrs. Pigeoncote *(to herself)***:** But Wilfrid the Snatcher is an orphan!

Mr. Pigeoncote *(to himself)*: We've got the wrong Wilfrid!

Wilfrid: I should have given the gift to you last night after dinner. But it's a silver cream jug, and you already have so many of them. I was planning to exchange it for another gift this morning — now it's gone.

Mr. Pigeoncote: Are you sure, Wilfrid, that you have a mother?

Wilfrid: What an odd question. Of course I have a mother. She is on vacation in Egypt. She wrote to me when I was in Germany, reminding me of your anniversary.

Mrs. Pigeoncote *(whispering to her husband)*: He was in Germany! This is the Wilfrid — the good Wilfrid — who is a diplomat!

Mr. Pigeoncote *(whispering to his wife)*: We're ruined!

Mrs. Pigeoncote *(to Wilfrid)*: How terrible to think we have a thief! Wait here!

Narrator: Mrs. Pigeoncote rushes into the next room and returns with a silver cream jug.

Mrs. Pigeoncote: There were seven cream jugs last night — and now there are eight.

Mr. Pigeoncote: What a curious trick of memory, Wilfrid! You must have slipped downstairs last night, put the silver jug with the others, then clean forgot about it.

Wilfrid *(inspecting the jug)*: This certainly is the jug I brought to you. It was in my suitcase this morning. I saw it there when I took out my bathrobe. Someone stole the jug from my room while I was taking a bath!

Narrator: The Pigeoncotes turn paler than ever. Then Mrs. Pigeoncote has an inspiration.

Mrs. Pigeoncote: Oh, dear! I'm feeling faint. Please fetch me my smelling salts.

Mr. Pigeoncote *(relieved to leave the room)*: Right away, my dear!

Mrs. Pigeoncote: Wilfrid, I'm glad we're alone. And I'm glad you work as a diplomat, since you will know how to handle this — er — awkward situation.

Wilfrid: What situation is that?

Mrs. Pigeoncote: It has to do with my husband's little problem. . . .

Wilfrid: Good Lord! Do you mean to say he's a kleptomaniac, like Wilfrid the Snatcher?

Mrs. Pigeoncote: Oh, he's not that bad. He won't snatch anything in plain sight. But he can't resist going through a locked suitcase! It's a special kind of kleptomania. The doctor's have a name for it.

Wilfrid: I'm so sorry.

Mrs. Pigeoncote: He must have raided your suitcase the second he saw it lying in your room. Of course, he had no motive for taking the cream jug —we already have seven.

Wilfrid: Say no more. I understand.

Narrator: Mr. Pigeoncote returns with the smelling salts.

Mrs. Pigeoncote *(to her husband)*: It's all right. I've explained everything. Don't say anything more about it.

Mr. Pigeoncote *(relieved)*: Whew! Brave little woman. I could never have explained it!

Scene Four

Narrator: Months later, the Pigeoncotes are visited by a Mrs. Consuelo Von Bullyon. Mr. Pigeoncote meets her in the hall on her way to the bathroom.

Mr. Pigeoncote: Good morning!

Mrs. Von Bullyon: Good morning.

Mr. Pigeoncote: What's that you're carrying? It's your suitcase! Why do you need your suitcase in the bathroom?

Mrs. Von Bullyon *(flustered)*: What? Oh, never mind!

Narrator: She rushes into the bathroom and slams the door.

Mr. Pigeoncote *(shaking his head)*: I will never understand women. Every woman who visits our house carries her suitcase into the bathroom!

Saki...

...is the penname of British author Hector Hugh Munro. Munro was born in 1870 in Burma, where his father served as a senior police official in the British colony. Munro was educated in England and, as a young man, returned to Burma where he followed in his father's footsteps on the colonial police force.

Poor health caused his early retirement, so Munro turned his hand to writing. He wrote political satire, and served as a newspaper correspondent. His first collection of short stories was published in 1904. He wrote four collections of stories in all, along with two novels. When World War I broke out in 1914, Munro enlisted in the British Army. He was killed in the trenches on November 13, 1916.

Saki's short stories are best known for their arch satirical portraits of British life as well as their patented ironic endings. His portrayals of life in English country houses were models for writers as diverse as humorist P.G. Wodehouse, novelist Evelyn Waugh, and mystery writer Agatha Christie.

FURTHER READING

For more of Saki's arch, ironic stories, read the chilling "Gabriel-Ernest" or "The She-Wolf" (both about werewolves!), "The Reticence of Lady Ann" or "Quail Seed."

 Young readers with a taste for British humor and well-constructed tales will also enjoy the work of P.G. Wodehouse — especially the adventures of Bertie Wooster and his unflappable valet, Jeeves.

ACTIVITIES

Double Standards

In this story, Saki is making fun of snobbery. The Pigeoncotes disliked their cousin Wilfrid when he was poor, but now that he has inherited money they are ready to excuse his faults. The Pigeoncotes have double standards — one they use for rich people, and another for everyone else.

Discuss the concept of double standards with students. Ask them if they can think of any examples of double standards in the contemporary world. Challenge students to identify any double standards they personally might hold. Have students explain if they think a double standard is ever justified.

The Snatcher

Wilfrid, the Pigeoncotes' house guest in this story, has a strange experience during his visit. Ask students to imagine they are Wilfrid writing a letter to his mother, describing the incident of the seven cream jugs. Would he be cruel in his descriptions? Would he try to sugarcoat the story? Students should choose a tone and stick to it as they tell all about Wilfrid's stay.

My Mystery

"The Seven Cream Jugs" is a classic case of mistaken identity. The Pigeoncotes assume their guest is "Wilfrid the Snatcher," and end up stealing themselves.

Have students write their own mystery using mistaken identity. They may use situations such as:

◆ a substitute teacher whom everyone assumes is mean
◆ a new kid in school with the same last name as a baseball star
◆ a teen who is the exact double for the President's kid

Introduction

The heroes in Dashiell Hammett's detective stories are called "hardboiled." Like an egg that has been boiled too long, they are tough and resilient. Tough, hardboiled heroes are still popular in crime movies and books around the world.

"The Tenth Clew" (Hammett spelled the word "clue" an old-fashioned way) is a classic hardboiled detective story. The hero, a fellow who works for the Continental Detective Agency, never tells us his own name. He's simply known as the Continental Op — short for "Operative," which is another word for worker. He's just a regular guy trying to do his job — a job that involves murder and mystery.

THE TENTH CLEW

By Dashiell Hammett

Characters

The Continental Op ("Op"), *a private detective for the Continental Detective Agency — no one knows his real name*

Charles Gantvoort, *a wealthy young man*

O'Gar, *a police detective*

Creda Dexter, *a beautiful young woman*

Madden Dexter, *Creda's older brother*

Smith, *a muscular young man*

Butler

Man

Narrator, *the narrator is the Continental Op, looking back on the case*

Scene One

Narrator: It was just after nine o'clock in the evening when I arrived at the Gantvoort house. A butler met me at the door.

Butler: Mr. Leopold Gantvoort is not at home. But his son, Charles, is available, if you would care to see him.

Op: No, I had an appointment with Mr. Leopold Gantvoort for nine or a little after. No doubt he'll be back soon. I'll wait for him.

Butler: Very well, sir. You may wait in the library.

Op: I waited for an hour. Then another. A clock somewhere had just begun to strike eleven when a young man came into the room.

Charles: My father hasn't returned yet. I'm sorry you have been kept waiting. Is there anything I can do for you? I'm Charles Gantvoort.

Op: No, thank you. I'll get in touch with your father tomorrow.

Narrator: Charles was showing me to the door when the telephone rang. His back was to me when he answered it.

Charles (*into the phone*): Yes. . . Yes. . . What?

Narrator: He turned to me, his face pale with shock.

Charles: Father is dead — killed.

Op: Where? How?

Charles: I don't know. That was the police. They want me to come down at once. If you will pardon me —

Op: Mr. Gantvoort, I am a detective for the Continental Detective Agency. Your father called up this afternoon and asked that a detective be sent to see him tonight. He said his life had been threatened. He had not officially hired us, though, so —

Charles: I'm hiring you right now! If the police haven't already caught the killer, I want you to do everything possible to catch him.

Op: All right! Let's get down to police headquarters.

Scene Two

Narrator: A half dozen detectives were waiting for us when we reached police headquarters. The officer in charge was named O'Gar — we had worked on two or three jobs together before, and hit it off excellently. We met in a small office. Spread out on the desk were a dozen or so things.

O'Gar: Mr. Gantvoort, I want you to look these things over carefully and pick out the ones that belonged to your father.

Narrator: I made a list of the things on the table while Charles Gantvoort made his selections.

Op (*to himself*): An empty jewel case, a memo book, three letters addressed to the dead man, a bunch of keys, a pen, two handkerchiefs, two bullets, a gold watch, two black wallets, some money, and a typewriter.

Charles: This watch, pen, memo book, letters, and wallet all belonged to my father.

O'Gar: Are you sure none of these other things are his?

Charles: No, I'm not certain. But I've never seen any of it before.

Op: Is anything that your father usually carried with him missing from among these things?

Charles: No. These are all of the things he would carry with him.

Op: At what time did he leave the house tonight?

Charles: Before seven-thirty. *(He blushes.)* I'm not sure, but I suppose he was going to call on Miss Dexter.

O'Gar: Who is she?

Charles: She's — well — father was on very friendly terms with Miss Dexter and her brother. He usually visited them in the evening. I believe father was intending to marry her.

O'Gar: What do you know about the Dexters?

Charles: Not much. Father got to know them about six months ago. Miss Dexter — her first name is Creda — is about 23 years old. Her brother Madden is about five years older. He is in New York now. My father sent him there on some business.

O'Gar: Did your father tell you he was going to marry Miss Dexter?

Dexter: No, but I feared as much.

Op: What do you mean, "feared?"

Charles: I don't want to make you suspect them. I'm sure they had nothing to do with father's murder. But I didn't especially like them. I thought they were just after my father's money.

Op: What about your father's will?

Charles: The last will I saw left everything to me and my wife. He may have made a new will — I don't really know.

O'Gar: Hmmm. We'll look into that. *(to Op)* Any other questions you want to ask?

Op: Yes. Mr. Gantvoort, did your father ever tell you anything about a man named Emil Bonfils?

Charles: No.

Op: Was your father ever in Paris?

Charles: Yes. He went there on business.

O'Gar: Why do you ask?

Op: Because Leopold Gantvoort called our agency this afternoon to say he had received a letter from a man named Emil Bonfils. Bonfils claimed they had met in Paris, and threatened to kill Leopold Gantvoort. That's why I was calling on Mr. Gantvoort — to protect him from Emil Bonfils!

Scene Three

Narrator: We let Charles Gantvoort go.

Op: Don't you think it's time you loosened up and told me the facts of the case?

O'Gar: I guess so. A grocer named Lagerquist was driving through Golden Gate Park tonight. He passed a car parked on a dark road. Lagerquist thought the guy sitting behind the wheel looked odd, so he reported it to a patrolman. The patrolman investigated and found Leopold Gantvoort behind the wheel of the car — dead. He had been smashed in the head by this.

Op *(surprised)*: The typewriter?

O'Gar: Yes. And all this stuff on the desk was scattered about in the car. Look at this letter we found in the car.

Op *(reading)*: "Gantvoort — I want what is mine. 6,000 miles and 21 years is not enough to hide you from the victim of your treachery. I want what you have stole. Signed, Emil Bonfils."

O'Gar: That must be the letter that made the dead man call you.

Op: Has to be. Did you find anything else in the car that's not on the desk?

O'Gar: This.

Narrator: It was a tuft of blond hair.

Op: This has been cut from someone's head — it wasn't pulled out.

O'Gar: That's right. And this was in one of the wallets.

Narrator: It was a sheet of paper. Neatly typed on it were the names and addresses of six people. The addresses were for cities all across the United States. The first name on the list was Leopold Gantvoort.

Op: This could be a list of potential murder victims.

O'Gar: That's what I thought.

Op: Anything else?

O'Gar: Only this. The dead man's left shoe was missing!

Op *(shaking his head)*: This is the screwiest murder I ever saw.

O'Gar: What do you think we should do?

Op: I think we should find Mr. Emil Bonfils. I'll have our agency's detective in Paris start looking on that end.

O'Gar: Good idea. In the meantime, I'll get in touch with all of the people on this list. It's too late for Leopold Gantvoort —but maybe we can prevent another murder!

Scene Four

Narrator: The next morning I returned to O'Gar's office. On the desk were a shoe, some rumpled newspaper, and a tiny key.

Op: What are these — souvenirs?

O'Gar: Might as well be. They were found in the lobby of a hotel downtown this morning. This is Gantvoort's missing shoe. It was wrapped up in the newspaper. Look — the heel is missing. This key was inside the shoe.

Op: What does the key open?

O'Gar: Your guess is as good as mine.

Op: This newspaper is from Philadelphia.

O'Gar: Yeah, but it was on sale at the hotel newsstand.

Op: Nothing about this case adds up!

O'Gar: I agree. While we wait to see if your man in Paris can give us a lead on Emil Bonfils, what do you say we pay a visit to the dead man's girlfriend?

Op: That's just what I was going to suggest.

Scene Five

Narrator: We went to the Dexters' apartment. It was a few blocks from the Gantvoort house. Creda Dexter was a pretty, cat-like young woman.

Creda: Mr. Gantvoort and I were to have been married the day after tomorrow.

Op: His son didn't tell us that.

Creda: He didn't know. He would not have approved of our marriage. Neither did my brother, Madden. That's why Leopold sent him to New York on business — to get Madden out of the way until we were on our honeymoon.

Op: Did Leopold Gantvoort visit you last night?

Creda: No. I was expecting him at about eight. When he was late, I called his house. The butler told me that Leopold had left earlier. But he never arrived. Then, this morning, I saw the newspapers —

Narrator: She bit her lip, as if holding back a sob. It was the only emotion she showed.

Op: Did Leopold ever mention to you that his life had been threatened?

Creda: No.

Op: Do you know Emil Bonfils?

Creda: No.

O'Gar: At what hotel is your brother staying in New York?

Narrator: A flash of fear passed over her pretty face.

Creda: I — I don't know.

O'Gar: When did he leave San Francisco?

Creda: Four days ago. He was traveling by train, of course.

Op: That means if he is in New York now, then it would be impossible for him to have been in San Francisco last night.

O'Gar: I spoke with Leopold Gantvoort's lawyer this morning, Miss Dexter. Did you know he was changing his will? He wanted to leave you half of his fortune.

Creda: Leopold had mentioned something like that. But I thought that he had not signed the new will yet.

O'Gar: That's right. The old one is still in effect. That means his son is going to get all of the money — and you won't get a dime!

Scene Six

Narrator: O'Gar and I returned to the office, disappointed.

O'Gar: She knew that the new will was not signed. That means she had no motive for killing the old man.

Op: I agree. Her brother, who is in New York, is also in the clear, since it's physically impossible for him to have been here.

O'Gar: Any luck tracking down Emil Bonfils?

Op: None. Our man in Paris says he can't find any trace of anyone by that name.

O'Gar: And we've been checking out the other names on this list of "victims" we found in the car. Get this — most of them don't exist!

Op: You're kidding. The people don't exist?

O'Gar: Not only that — the addresses don't either. They're all made up! This is one funny case.

Op: It is. We got nine clews, and none of them add up to a thing. Let's go over them.

O'Gar: Clew number one —the murdered man called up your detective agency to say he had received a threatening letter from a man named Emil Bonfils.

Op: Number two —the man was killed with this typewriter —as screwy a weapon as you can hope to find.

O'Gar: Number three —there were two bullets in the car.

Op: Number four —there was also an empty jewel case.

O'Gar: Number five —we also found a bunch of yellow hair.

Op: Number six —the dead man's shoe was missing.

O'Gar: Number seven —two wallets were in the car

Op: Number eight —this list of names was inside one of the wallets.

O'Gar: Number nine —the missing shoe turned up in a hotel lobby, along with a rusty old key, the next day.

Op: What does it all mean?

O'Gar: Here's what I think. I think this Emil Bonfils picked up Leopold last night in a car and took him to the park. Then he bashed Leopold in the noodle with this typewriter, dropped the bullets and jewelry case, and then stole the man's shoe. But . . . what about this list of names? It doesn't make any sense!

Op *(excited)*: You're right —it doesn't make sense! And if those names are all fake —I'll bet that the rest of those clews are cooked-up, too!

O'Gar: But . . . why?

Op: Whoever left these clews wants us to look for "Emil Bonfils." The clews point to a man from Paris with light hair, who carries a gun, and had a grudge against Leopold Gantvoort. It's all a bum steer! From now on, I'm going to do look for someone just the opposite of who these clews point to!

Stop!
You be the Detective!
If all of the clews are "red herrings" intended to distract you from the real criminal, then whom do you think is the prime suspect?

- ◆ Charles Gantvoort, who inherited all of his father's money?
- ◆ Creda Dexter, who planned to marry the murdered man?
- ◆ Madden Dexter, who opposed his sister's marriage?
- ◆ Or could there be some other likely suspect?

Think about whom you think is most suspicious. List the suspects' motives — and their alibis. Think about how you would proceed if you were the detective.
Then read on!

Scene Seven

Narrator: A few days later, Madden Dexter was due back from New York. His train was passing through Sacramento. I had a few questions for Madden, so I went to Sacramento and boarded his train there. I gave a porter my card and told him to deliver it to Madden Dexter. I followed the porter through the train as he called out the name. Near the rear of the train, a slim, shifty-looking young man looked up.

Madden: I am Madden Dexter.

Narrator: I sat next to him and smiled.

Madden: I suppose you want to see me about Mr. Gantvoort's death?

Op: That's right. I have a few questions.

Madden: I'm happy to help. But I already told the detectives in New York everything I know.

Op: I have a few special questions. They are about your sister. . .

Madden: I'm sure she had nothing to do with it!

Op: That's good to hear. But I was wondering whether or not she had any old boyfriends who might not be so innocent. . . .

Madden (*gulping*)**:** Boyfriends?

Op: That's right. She's a very pretty young woman. I was wondering if she had any boyfriends who might be jealous that she was planning to marry an older man like Mr. Gantvoort.

Madden (*with conviction*)**:** I am quite certain that my sister never dated another man in her entire life!

Scene Eight

Narrator: I underestimated Madden Dexter. I thought he would crack under questioning. But for the entire trip he stuck by his story. His sister had no ex-boyfriends, he said. I was still suspicious, since his nervousness made me sure that Madden was covering up for someone.

Op: Well, the train stops here, in Oakland. We'll have to take the ferry across the bay to San Francisco.

Madden: Won't you leave me alone?

Op: Just a few more questions. . . .

Narrator: It was a dark, wet, foggy night. I followed Madden onto the crowded ferry boat. He walked up to a tall, muscular young man wearing an overcoat.

Madden: Hello, Smith!

Smith: Who is your friend?

Madden: He's a detective.

Narrator: I immediately knew something was up. Before I could do anything, though, Smith was standing next to me. Something dug in my ribs. I looked down. Smith had a gun aimed point blank at my heart.

Smith: Let's go to the upper deck.

Op: Are you sure? It's cold and wet up there —

Smith (*threatening*)**:** Move.

Narrator: I went up to the top deck of the ferry boat. It was empty under the dark, foggy skies. By this time we were in the middle of San Francisco Bay.

Smith: Keep moving. Let's go someplace quiet, where we can talk.

Narrator: He prodded me to the rail at the stern of the boat. Suddenly, the entire back of my head burned with sudden fire . . . tiny points of light glittered in the blackness before me . . . grew larger . . . came rushing toward me . . . .

Scene Nine

Narrator: The next thing I knew my eyes burned with salt water and I was surrounded by freezing cold water. Fog horns blared in the distance. I was in the harbor, being carried out to sea by the current! I struggled to swim, but soon grew weary. My limbs were heavy. I was exhausted. All I wanted was to sleep. . . sleep. Then I saw a row of lights passing by. It was another ferry!

Op: Help! Help!

Narrator: Then everything went black.

Scene Ten

Narrator: I opened my eyes.

Op: Where am I?

Man: Sausalito. We fished you out of the bay as we passed by in the ferry. You're lucky to be alive! Just sit quiet till the ambulance shows up.

Op: When's the next boat leave for San Francisco?

Man: Five minutes.

Op: I've got to be on that boat!

Narrator: An hour later I was in my apartment, changing into dry clothes. I got on the phone. My first call was to Charles Gantvoort.

Charles: What can I do for you?

Op: Madden Dexter is back from New York.

Charles: I know. I spoke to him over the phone. We are going to meet tomorrow to discuss the business he did for father in New York.

Op: Call him back and tell him you have to see him tonight!

Charles: Why?

Op: I'll explain later. Meet me outside of his apartment in a half hour.

Narrator: Next, I called O'Gar. I explained what happened to me on the ferry.

O'Gar: It looks to me like this Mr. Smith is our man. He must be an old flame of Creda Dexter.

Op: That's what I figure. Let's hope he's still in town!

Narrator: Soon I met Charles Gantvoort and O'Gar in the lobby of the Dexters' apartment building. Charles rang the intercom.

Creda (*through the intercom*)**:** Who is it?

Charles: It's me, Creda. I'm here to see your brother.

Creda: Come on up.

Narrator: We made our way to the Dexter's apartment. I knocked on the door. It swung open and I stood face to face with —

Op: Smith!

Smith: You! I thought I finished you off on the boat!

Narrator: He reached into his coat. Before he could grab his gun, I shoved him. He fell over. In a flash, O'Gar and I had him pinned.

Op: Here's the killer —Smith.

Charles (*confused*)**:** Smith? Who is Smith?

Op: This man!

Charles: But —but, this is Madden Dexter!

Scene Eleven

Narrator: A few minutes later, O'Gar and I were questioning the man who had pushed me into the harbor —the man who turned out to be Madden Dexter.

Madden: Anything I have to say, I'll say to my lawyer!

Op: It's all right. I've got it all figured out, I guess.

O'Gar: Yeah?

Op: Sure. Madden Dexter had it in for Mr. Gantvoort. When the old man sent him to New York on business, he got someone else —that fellow I met on the train — to go in his place. Then Madden set up the crime by sending the fake letter from "Bonfils." After committing the murder, he left those other fake clews. All along, he had the perfect alibi for the crime. He was allegedly in New York — all the while he was here in San Francisco, killing his sister's fiancé.

Creda: He's not my brother.

Madden: You keep quiet!

Creda: Why should I? Me and Madden, we're not brother and sister. We're con artists. We hit on old Mr. Gantvoort thinking we could swindle him.

Charles: I knew you were up to something!

Creda: Yeah? Well, something funny happened along the way. The old guy fell in love with me.

Madden: Don't make me sick.

Creda: He did! And I fell for him, too. We really were going to get married.

Madden *(angry)*: You were just trying to cut me out of the action!

Creda: I would have taken care of you! But you're so greedy —you couldn't stand to see me quit the con game!

O'Gar: Who was the guy who went to New York, posing as your brother?

Creda: I'll bet anything it was Evan Felter. He's an old partner of ours. Odds are he's already hiding out in L.A. somewhere.

Narrator: And he was. A few months later, Felter was in jail for fraud. Madden Dexter was convicted of murder. Charles Gantvoort proved to be a decent fellow — he gave half his father's fortune to Creda Dexter, since that's how the old man wanted it. And Creda Dexter? She's a very respectable woman, now, and glad to be free of the con game.

Dashiell Hammett...

...was a unique mystery author — he actually worked as a private detective before becoming a writer!

Hammett was born in Maryland in 1894, and grew up there and in Pennsylvania. He left school at the age of 14 and held a number of odd jobs before finding work with the famous Pinkerton Detective Agency. Except for a brief stint in the Ambulance Corps of the U.S. Army during World War I, Hammett worked as a detective for the Pinkerton Agency until 1922, when he quit to become a writer. By this time, Hammett was living in San Francisco, the city that would be the setting for most of his stories.

Hammett is known for inventing the "hard-boiled" school of detective fiction. Unlike the elaborate puzzle-like stories of writers such as Ellery Queen or Agatha Christie, Hammett's mysteries are blunt, violent, "realistic" tales of greed, jealousy and political corruption. Hammett created a number of memorable detectives in his novels and short stories. The hero of

FURTHER READING

Students who enjoy this detective story may want to read some of Donald Sobol's Encyclopedia Brown books. In this series, the quick-witted boy nicknamed "Encyclopedia" helps his father, a police chief, solve baffling cases. Sobol won the Edgar Allan Poe Award from the Mystery Writers of America in 1976 for his entire body of work.

ACTIVITIES
Train Days

"The Tenth Clew" is set in the 1920s, before jet airplanes made it possible to travel across the country in a matter of hours. Ask students to research and list other inventions we have today that were not around back then (such as computers, television, satellites, compact disks, cellular phones, microwaves, and so on). Ask students which inventions on their lists have changed the world the most, and have them give reasons to support their answers.

Understanding Idioms

The phrase "red herring" is an example of an idiom. An idiom is an expression or phrase that means something different from what it appears to mean. Your students may be interested to know where the term "red herring" comes from. A herring is a fish that when pickled in a certain way turns red. Red herring has strong smell. Long ago, it was used to teach hunting dogs to follow a trail. It was dragged on the ground and the dogs followed its scent. Later, people who hated hunting dragged a red herring across the path of the fox the dogs were chasing. The dogs would get confused, stop following the fox, and follow the smell of the herring. Sometimes criminals being chased would also use red herrings to cover up their own scents so the bloodhounds chasing them would get confused.

Students may enjoy collecting other idioms and finding out how they came about. Create an "idiom wall" where students can post their findings. To get them started suggest the following idioms: *cry wolf*, *worth your salt*, and *watch your p's and q's*.

Where There's A Will...

This story features a will, which is a standard plot device in mystery stories.

Ask students to make up a will of their own. They may either make up a will leaving their current possessions to whomever they wish, or they can imagine that their wildest dreams have come true, they own everything they could ever wish for, and must decide to whom to leave it all.

When they are done, students may wish to share their wills with the class, explaining why they chose to leave their things to whom they did.

My Mystery

"The Tenth Clew" features red herrings — a device used by mystery writers in which readers are given false clues and suspects in order to confuse them.

Students may write their own mystery stories using red herrings. First, have them plot out a crime and its solution. Next, they should write a list of possible red herrings to confuse the reader. After they have plotted out the story and the false clues, students may write their stories.

Hammett (continued)
"The Tenth Clew" is the Continental Op — the nameless, world-weary hero of dozens of short stories and Hammett's first novel, *Red Harvest*. Hammett is perhaps best known for inventing Nick and Nora Charles (in *The Thin Man*) and Sam Spade (*The Maltese Falcon*). Each of these novels was adapted into a classic movie.

Hammett died in 1961, almost thirty years after his last books were written. Although he did not write his own works during the final decades of his life, Hammett served as inspiration and mentor to the world-renowned playwright Lillian Hellman.

AS SIMPLE AS ABC

By Ellery Queen

Introduction

"Ellery Queen" was king of the "who-dunit." A "whodunit" is a mystery story where the reader tries to guess "who done it," that is, who committed the crime. These stories, with their carefully-made plots and baffling clues, are almost like puzzles. Other famous "whodunit" authors include Agatha Christie, Rex Stout, and Ngaio Marsh.

In "As Simple as ABC," we work alongside Ellery Queen as he solves a crime over 70 years in the making. Set in the 1930's, the story involves buried treasure, Civil War veterans, and a lethal bugle.

Characters

Ellery Queen, *a private detective*

Nikki, *his secretary*

Dr. Strong, *a man in his sixties*

Cissy Chase, *a young woman, Abner Chase's great-grand-daughter*

Zach Bigelow, *a man in his late nineties*

Andy Bigelow, *Zach's grandson*

Abner Chase
Zach Bigelow } *three soldiers in the Civil War*
Caleb Atwell

Narrator

Scene One

Narrator: It is a Sunday in late May. Ellery Queen and his secretary, Nikki, are driving from Washington, D.C., back home to New York City. It is after dark and the pair are on a country road when it starts to rain. Their car breaks down.

Nikki: We're marooned!

Ellery: I'll get this car started again. . . hold on. Isn't that a house up ahead?

Nikki: Yes.

Ellery: Let's go. At least we'll find out where we are and how far it is to where we ought to be.

Narrator: Ellery and Nikki run to the old house and knock on the door. An elderly man, Dr. Martin Strong, answers the door and lets them in.

Ellery: Sorry to be a bother, but if I could use your phone to call a garage —

Dr. Strong: Don't be silly. You'll spend the night here. This storm's going to keep up all night long, and the roads here-about get mighty soupy. I'll have the garage fix your car in the morning.

Narrator: Ellery and Nikki look around. The house is neat and clean. A bright fire blazes in the fireplace. The rain outside comes down with a roar.

Ellery (*smiling*)**:** Thank you for your hospitality.

Scene Two

Narrator: An hour later, the three of them sit next to the cozy fire.

Nikki: So you're the doctor of Jacksburg, this small town.

Dr. Strong (*chuckling*)**:** Also the mayor and chief of police. A lot of us in this village have at least two jobs.

Ellery: To me you'll always be the Good Samaritan, Dr. Strong.

Dr. Strong: Call me Doc. Why, it's just selfishness on my part. We're off the beaten track here, and you do get a hankering for a new face. I guess I know every dimple and freckle on the five hundred and thirty-four folks in Jacksburg.

Ellery: I don't suppose your police work keeps you very busy.

Dr. Strong: Not at all. Though last year . . . (*a serious look crosses his face*) Did you say, Nikki, that Mr. Queen is sort of a detective?

Nikki: Sort of a detective? Why, he's simply brilliant!

Ellery (*blushing*)**:** I stick my nose into a case every once in a while. What about last year, Doc?

Dr. Strong: I may be a fool, but I'm worried.

Nikki: Worried about what?

Dr. Strong: Well, Memorial Day's tomorrow, and the first time in my life I'm not looking forward to it. Jacksburg makes quite a fuss about Memorial Day. It's not every village can brag about three living veterans of the Civil War.

Nikki: Three!

Dr. Strong: Gives you an idea of how much call for a doctor there is around these parts. Folks live a long time here. Anyway, I should have said we had three Civil War veterans. Caleb Atwell, age ninety-seven — Zach Bigelow, age ninety-five, who lives with his grandson Andy — and Abner Chase, ninety-four. Caleb Atwell died last Memorial Day.

Ellery: A, B, C. . . .

Dr. Strong: What's that?

Ellery: Their last names begin with A, B, and C. Atwell, Bigelow, and Chase. A died last Memorial Day. Is that what's worrying you? B following A?

Dr. Strong: Doesn't it always? But I'm afraid it isn't as simple as that. Every year, Caleb, Zach, and Abner were the stars of our Memorial Day services down at the cemetery. The oldest —

Ellery: That would be A. Caleb Atwell.

Dr. Strong: That's right. As the oldest, Caleb would always blow taps on his old bugle from the war. Zach Bigelow, as the next oldest, would carry the flag. Ab Chase, the youngest, he'd lay a wreath on the monument.

Nikki: What happened last year?

Dr. Strong: Caleb was blowing taps the way he'd been doing nigh unto twenty times before. All of a sudden, in the middle of a high note, Caleb keeled over. Dropped in his tracks. Deader than church on Monday.

Nikki: He strained himself. What a poetic way for a Civil War veteran to die.

Dr. Strong: Maybe. If you like that kind of poetry.

Ellery: Surely, Doc, you can't be suspicious about the death of man who was ninety-seven years old.

Dr. Strong: But I'd given him a check-up only the day before he died. I would have sworn he'd live to see one hundred — and then some!

Ellery: Hmmm. Why else do you suspect that Caleb was murdered, Doc?

Nikki: Was he rich?

Dr. Strong: No. Not unless the legend is true. Folks say that the three old-timers found a treasure way back during the Civil War.

Nikki (*incredulous*)**:** A treasure?

Dr. Strong: Yep. Legend has it they found a treasure, brought it back here to Jacksburg, and buried it. The last surviving one of the three gets to keep it all!

Ellery: Doc, that's a common tale. Lots of old men tell stories like that, just to keep young whippersnappers like us entertained.

Dr. Strong: I know, I know! Just the same, I'll breathe a lot easier when tomorrow's ceremonies are over and old Zach Bigelow lays that bugle aside for another year!

Scene Three

Narrator: The next morning, Ellery and Nikki meet in Dr. Strong's kitchen. The doctor is cooking breakfast.

Dr. Strong: Morning. Just fixing your breakfast before I catch an hour's nap.

Nikki: Thank you, Doc. Didn't you sleep well last night?

Dr. Strong: Didn't sleep at all. I was just dropping off when the phone rang. It was Cissy Chase. An emergency sick call.

Ellery: Cissy Chase? Wasn't Chase the name you mentioned last night?

Dr. Strong: Yes, she's old Abner Chase's great-granddaughter. That's right, Mr. Queen. Cissy's an orphan and Ab's only kin. She's kept house for the old fellow and taken care of him since she was ten.

Ellery: Was she calling about old Abner?

Dr. Strong (*sadly*)**:** I was up with Ab all night. This morning, at six thirty, he passed away.

Nikki (*quietly*)**:** On Memorial Day.

Narrator: They all fall silent for a minute.

Ellery: What did Abner Chase die of?

Dr. Strong: A stroke. That's as close to a natural cause as you come with a man his age. No, there wasn't any funny business about this death.

Ellery: Except it happened on Memorial Day . . . . I wonder how old Zach Bigelow's going to take the news?

Dr. Strong: He's already taken it, Mr. Queen. I stopped in at Andy Bigelow's place on my way home. Figured I best let old Zach know as soon as possible.

Nikki: Poor thing. I wonder how it feels to learn you're the only one left?

Dr. Strong: Can't say Zach carried on about it. About all he said was, "Doggone it, now who's goin' to lay the wreath after I toot the bugle?"

Scene Four

Narrator: Ellery and Nikki visit Cissy Chase. The house she shared with her great-grandfather is small and dreary, with a dark and musty-smelling parlor. Cissy herself is a plain young woman of about twenty.

Nikki: You poor dear. May I call you Cissy?

Cissy: I suppose.

Ellery: I understand the Memorial Day parade is going to start outside your house, Cissy. Have Andy Bigelow and his grandfather Zach arrived yet?

Cissy: I don't know. It's all like such a dream, seems like.

Ellery: Of course it does. And you're all alone. Haven't you got any family left at all, Cissy?

Cissy: No.

Nikki: You must have a boyfriend.

Cissy: Who'd want to go out with me? I don't have any nice clothes or things. We lived off great-grandpa's pension — and what I could earn doing day jobs around town, which isn't much.

Nikki: I'm sure you'll find something to do.

Cissy: In Jacksburg?

Ellery: Cissy, Doc Strong told us about a treasure. Do you know anything about it?

Cissy (*smiling*): Oh, that. All I know is what great-grandpa told me, and he never told the same story twice. As near as I can make out, during the Civil War, him, Caleb Atwell, and Zach Bigelow were on a scouting mission. . .

Scene Five

Narrator: We flash back to the Civil War. Young Ab, Caleb, and Zach are hiding in the ruined basement of a southern plantation.

Ab: Fellas! Look over here!

Caleb: What did you find, Ab?

Ab: A metal box. It's got a lock on it. Do you think it might hold something valuable?

Zach: Only one way to find out!

Narrator: He takes out his gun and shoots the lock off the box. Ab opens it up.

Ab: Holy cats!

Caleb: It's money!

Zach: A fortune! What'll we do with it? Take it with us?

Ab: We'd never make it through the enemy lines carrying this much money. Let's bury it here.

Caleb: Good idea. After the war, we'll come back for it.

Zach: Then what? Should we split it three ways?

Ab: I've got a better idea. Let's keep all the money together, then the last one of us to survive will get to keep it all!

Scene Six

Narrator: We are back in Cissy's parlor.

Ellery: That's quite a story your great-grandpa told. Did he ever mention how much money they found?

Cissy *(chuckling)*: A couple hundred thousand dollars.

Nikki: You sound as if you don't believe the story.

Cissy: Now, I ain't saying great-grandpa was cracked. But — you know how an old man gets.

Ellery: Did he ever tell you where he hid the money?

Cissy: No, he'd just slap his knee and wink at me.

Ellery *(to Nikki)*: Hmmm. Maybe there's something to this yarn after all.

Nikki: If there is, then that old scoundrel Zach Bigelow has been murdering his friends to get the money!

Ellery: After all of these years? At the age of ninety-five? I wonder. . . .

Scene Seven

Narrator: Soon a crowd of people have gathered outside the house. The parade is about to start. Old Zach Bigelow is sitting in a place of honor in the first car. His grandson Andy, a rough-looking man, stands alongside.

Ellery *(to Andy)*: How do I address your grandfather, Mr. Bigelow?

Andy: Gramp's a general. Ain't you Gramp? *(to Ellery)* He actually went through the war a private, but we don't like to talk about that.

Ellery *(to Zach)*: General Bigelow —

Zach: Hey? Speak up, bub! Ye're mumblin'.

Ellery: General Bigelow, now that all of the money is yours, what will you do with it?

Zach: Hey? Money?

Andy: The treasure, Gramp! Even these strangers have heard about it! He wants to know what you are going to do with it.

Zach: Does, does he?

Ellery: How much money does it amount to, General?

Zach: Mighty nosy, ain't ye? Last time we counted it, it came to nigh on a million dollars. Yes, sir, one million dollars. Goin' to be a big surprise to the smart-alecks and doubtin' Thomases, just you wait and see!

Nikki *(to Dr. Strong)*: According to Cissy, Abner Chase said it was only two hundred thousand dollars.

Dr. Strong: Zach makes it more every time he talks about it.

Zach: I heard that! I'll show you, you young whippersnapper!

Dr. Strong: Now, Zach, save your breath for the bugle!

Narrator: The parade to the cemetery begins.

Scene Eight

Narrator: The parade makes it to the cemetery. The entire town watches as old Zach Bigelow stands by the Civil War memorial.

Andy *(yelling)*: Go ahead, Gramp!

Zach: I'm havin' trouble getting the durn bugle out of this sack.

Andy: Let me help.

Dr. Strong *(quietly)*: Let the old man alone, Andy. We're in no hurry.

Narrator: At last, Zach gets the ancient, dented bugle from the sack. He slowly puts it to his lips and begins to blow. At first, a few cracked sounds come from the horn. Then old Zach's face turns red. His eyes pop out. The bugle drops from his hand and the old man collapses to the ground. Dr. Strong, Nikki, and Ellery rush to the old man's side.

Dr. Strong: Zach! Zach! Speak to me!

Nikki: Is he all right, doctor?

Ellery: Or is he — is he? . . .

Dr. Strong *(sadly)*: Jacksburg's last Civil War veteran has gone to his final resting place.

Scene Nine

Narrator: Hours later, Ellery, Nikki, Dr. Strong, and Andy are in the Bigelows' living room.

Ellery: Your suspicions about last year were right, Doc.

Doc Strong: I should have checked that bugle!

Ellery: It's not an easy poison to spot, Doc.

Doc: They're all gone. All three. Who could have poisoned that bugle?

Andy: Well, don't look at me! Anybody could have done it.

Doc: Anybody? The bugle was in your house all year long!

Andy: And it hung on our mantle. Anyone could have snuck in and poisoned it. Beside, who poisoned it last year, when it was at old Caleb's house?

Ellery: Bigelow, did your grandfather ever let on where that Civil War treasure is?

Andy: What if he did?

Ellery: That money is behind these murders, Bigelow.

Andy: I don't know anything about that. Anyway, no one has any right to that money except me. When Ab Chase died this morning, Gramp was the last survivor. The money was his — and I'm his next of kin, so the money's mine!

Dr. Strong: You know where it's hid, Andy. I'm the chief of police here, and this is a murder case. Where is that money?

Andy: All right. Gramp wrote me a note just as soon as he heard that Ab Chase had died.

Narrator: He hands Dr. Strong a piece of paper.

Zach's Voice (*reading*): "Dear Andy, Now that Ab Chase is dead too — if something happens to me you will find the money we've been keeping all these long years in an iron box in the coffin we buried Caleb Atwell in. I leave it all to you since you've been such a good grandson to me. Yours truly, Zach Bigelow."

Scene Ten

Narrator: Dr. Strong leads a group of men to dig up Caleb Atwell's grave. In the coffin they find an iron box with a lock on it. They bring it back to town, where Doctor Strong opens it. . . .

Dr. Strong (*gasps, looking in the box*): Would you look at all that money . . . .

Ellery: And it's all worthless!

Andy: What do you mean?

Ellery: Look! These are Confederate dollars! It was during the Civil War, remember? These dollars are interesting souvenirs, but they have no value as money at all!

Dr. Strong: I don't understand.

Ellery: It was a private joke among the three old rascals. For years, they told everyone they had a "fortune," but never let on that it was in Confederate money. Then, when Caleb died last year, the other two decided to slip it in to his casket, so that he could have the honor of keeping it. He was the oldest one, after all.

Dr. Strong: But — what about the poisoned bugles? This doesn't explain the murders at all.

Ellery: Well, now, Doc, it does. I know who killed these fine old men — and why.

Stop!
Can you solve the case?
You have heard and seen everything Ellery Queen has. See if you can solve the case alongside him. Ask yourself:

◆ What crimes have been committed?
◆ Who is the criminal?
◆ And what was the motive?

Hint: It's as simple as ABC.
Do you have the answers? Read on to see if you are right!

Scene Eleven

Narrator: Ellery, Nikki, Dr. Strong, and Andy Bigelow meet on the porch of Cissy Chase's house.

Ellery: There's no trick to this. The answer is as simple as the initials on their last names. Who knew that the "fortune" was in Confederate money, and thus worthless?

Nikki: No one but the three old men themselves.

Ellery: Exactly. And they would not have planned and committed murders in order to get the worthless money. Thus, the killer was someone who thought the fortune was real, and also thought he could claim it legally. Who would be able to claim the fortune legally when the last of the three old men had died?

Dr. Strong: The last survivor's heir.

Ellery: And who is the last survivor's heir?

Dr. Strong: Zach Bigelow's grandson, Andy!

Narrator: Andy tries to hide behind Cissy Chase, who steps aside.

Cissy (*scornful*): You thought the fortune was real! So you killed Caleb Atwell and my great-grandpa so your grandfather'd be the last survivor — so you could kill him and get the fortune!

Nikki: That's it!

Ellery: There's more to it than that, I'm afraid. You all refer to Zach Bigelow as the last survivor.

Nikki: Well, he was.

Dr. Strong: Of course he was! Caleb and Abner died first.

Ellery: Literally that's true. But you are all forgetting that Zach Bigelow was the last survivor only by accident. You said it yourself, Doc. Abner Chase died of natural causes. Don't you see? If Abner had not died this morning, he'd still be alive this afternoon! Zach Bigelow would have put the bugle to his lips — just as Caleb Atwell did one year ago . . . and at this moment, Abner Chase would be the last survivor.

Dr. Strong: I see! And who was Abner Chase's only living heir?

Narrator: Cissy Chase blushes and looks away.

Ellery: You lied to me earlier, Cissy. You pretended you didn't believe the story of the fortune. But that was just after your great-grandfather inconsiderately died of a stroke — a few hours before old Zach would die of poisoning, and you couldn't inherit that great, great fortune anyway!

"Ellery Queen"...

...was "born" in 1929. Two young businessmen, cousins Frederick Dannay and Manfred B. Lee, wrote a mystery novel, *The Roman Hat Mystery*. The hero of the story was a young mystery writer named Ellery Queen. The authors decided to use their character's name as their pen name.

Over the years, Dannay and Lee wrote hundreds of mystery stories, both short stories and novels. Their fictional detective, Ellery Queen, also became a popular radio character.

In 1941 — 100 years after Edgar Allan Poe invented the detective story — Dannay and Lee founded *The Ellery Queen Mystery Magazine* (EQMM). "As Simple as ABC" first appeared in EQMM in 1951. To this day, the magazine publishes the best detective and mystery fiction. Many of the world's top mystery authors were first published in EQMM.

FURTHER READING

"Ellery Queen" authored literally hundreds of short stories and novels, many of which may be found in public libraries.

Students with a taste for "whodunits" will want to read the work of Agatha Christie, the best-known and best-loved of all mystery writers.

 Mystery-lovers of all ages should find copies of the Ellery Queen Mystery Magazine which, after 55 years, still publishes the best short mystery fiction.

ACTIVITIES

Old Soldiers

This story is set in the 1930s, when the last survivors of the Civil War were still alive. Point out to students that Memorial Day is a day to honor soldiers who fought and died in wars. Ask students to name the wars since the 1930s in which American soldiers have fought. Students may conduct oral interviews with parents or grandparents to learn their memories of events during World War II, the Korean War, the Vietnam War, or the Gulf War.

"I Confess"

Ellery Queen solves the case through logic and because he understands Cissy Chase's motive. Ask students to assume the role of Cissy Chase. Have them re-read the play, paying special attention to Cissy's speeches in scene four. Then have each student write a confession in Cissy's voice, stating her motives for committing the murders.

My Mystery

"As Simple as ABC" is an example of a tontine mystery. In a tontine, a group of people share a fortune, agreeing that the last survivor gets to keep the entire amount. The premise has been used in many murder mystery novels and such classic mystery movies as *Charade* and *The List of Adrian Messenger*.

Have students write their own variation on the tontine theme. Their mysteries can use the following situations:

◆ a group of kids sharing a cabin at summer camp find a Native American artifact

◆ a team of kids working on a science project win a computer as a prize

◆ a group of Scouts find a rare fossil while hiking

NOTES

NOTES

NOTES